Elizabeth is a president of non-profit organisation "Information is Power," a teacher, an advisor, an activist, and a writer of other bestselling books; *The Cultural Qualities You Must Acquire to Succeed in Higher Education*, *The Principles That Facilitate Successful and Timely Degree Completion* and *Integrering Er Informasjon*. Her books deliver diverse practical information that has helped people change their perceptions and practices in academic and non-academic contexts. She has also written other books, *Articulating Research Students' Expectations of a Competent Supervisor* and *The Skills Required of Research Students in Academic Supervision*, which will be released soon. Elizabeth aims at supporting higher education stakeholders with information, as she believes reliable, relevant, and timely information is the power to support people. Besides, higher education student attrition is a challenging problem that requires collective supportive strategies such as those written in Elizabeth's books. The books are vital for all higher education stakeholders, including students, supervisors, advisors, parents, donor agencies, governments, and policymakers.

Indeed, information is power for all, including you.

This book is dedicated to my children and to all higher education stakeholders.

Elizabeth Paradiso Urassa

ALL YOU NEED TO KNOW BEFORE COMMENCING HIGHER EDUCATION

AUSTIN MACAULEY PUBLISHERS™

LONDON ∗ CAMBRIDGE ∗ NEW YORK ∗ SHARJAH

A CIP catalogue record for this title is available from the British Library.

ISBN 9781528999892 (Paperback)
ISBN 9781528999908 (ePub e-book)

www.austinmacauley.com

First Published 2023
Austin Macauley Publishers Ltd®
1 Canada Square
Canary Wharf
London
E14 5AA

I would like to express my special gratitude to my family, especially my children Colin, EshiDoreen, and Calvin. You always help me motivate myself, and it is lovely having you around me and be able to have operational schedules. Thank you very much.

Second, I want to thank all the academics and students who support me with information concerning higher education structure and practices. Specifically, my gratitude goes to Pro. David Hansen for shaping my thoughts and reviewed my work. Others are Moshi and Gasper Christopher Magnar for their narratives that can be a lesson to others.

Moreover, I would also like to thank all other participants who provided me with information; although you do want your names to appear in this book, I will not forget you, and indeed, it could be hard to write this book without your support.

Lastly, I would like to thank the Austin Macauley Publishers for their professional work in the harsh circumstances of coronavirus facing the world today. Your effort in editing, designing, and publishing this book is unforgettable and fantastic; thank you very much.

Last and not least, I thank all the readers for choosing this book; I believe many people desire to join higher education due to coronavirus, which has made them lose their jobs. Therefore reading the book before commencing the studies can benefit you in comprehending what to anticipate. You may also find it relevant to reading the other two books listed on the next page.

Definition of Terms

Acculturation – Is a process where students modify their values, norms, and culture to adjust themselves to a new learning environment while modifying the culture of their learning environment.

Academic – Refers to a university teacher or a scholar who has qualifications recognized by HEIs and who may carry supervision responsibilities for HE students. It also means the educational and learned person or a group. The term is used interchangeably with a supervisor and faculty.

A Leader – Is an individual who has the responsibility to guide others to attain the expected goals. In this book, learning agencies are leaders who lead students learning, and their primary function is to motivate, cooperate, inspire, empower and be a role model to the students toward attaining their learning goals.

A research Degree – Is an advanced learning programme that provides students with the freedom to choose the topic or problem of their interest and devote their time to solving the problem through scientific investigation. The research students are expected to produce new knowledge and expertise that is appropriate, rational, and innovative.

Competencies – are the ability to perform a task of multitasking or the capability to solve a problem (s) effectively by utilising sets of skills and knowledge.

Culture – Is a term that defines values, norms, social life activities of a particular group of people and that construct and defines them differently from other groups.

Digital /Distance Learning – This is a system of learning where learners and teachers interact through technology (electronic devices, tools, systems, and resources) and the courses are facilitated by technology through online programmes and mediums (social media, Bloggs, and some specific university me) out of the natural setting.

Enculturation – Is the process by which students learn by observation in a flexible and natural setting to acquire norms, values, and culture required or practiced adjusting and fit in the learning environment.

Gender – A masculine and feminine nature of humanity that is recognised by society and culturally constructed and is applied when defining individuals' role in a society regardless of sex, physiological and biological characteristics.

Graduates – Are successful research degree students in bachelor, master's, and doctoral levels of education who have acquired a degree. Although in normal circumstances, bachelor students are undergraduate while the master's and doctoral students are graduates, in this book, all who have a research degree are regarded as graduates.

Knowledge – Is an understanding or awareness that originates from intuition, learning, observation, and experiences that lead to the acquisition of certain skills that support an individual in performing specific or general tasks.

Inclusive Pedagogy – This is a kind of learning and teaching process that acknowledges diverse learning environments, ideas, and styles. Learners' and teachers' social values, beliefs, and needs are the vital part of the learning process where learning recognizes the individuality of learners' needs, understanding, contributions, and realities.

Leadership – Is a state of psychosocial influence that legitimises an individual(s) to lead, guide, and direct another/other individuals, group of people, and an organisation(s) to attain specific goals. The main aim is to enhance and support subordinates' efforts to attain personal and organizational (institutional) goals that cannot be achieved without guidance and support.

Learning – Is the process of acquiring new knowledge or modifying the existed knowledge, values, and skills through personal initiatives, friends, family, and experiences (informal) or a structured and organised learning system of schooling with the help of teachers, curriculum, and other learning agencies in a formal setting.

Learning agencies – Are the collection of individuals and supporters who facilitate students' learning in HE. It may be peers, friends, administrators, librarians, tutors, and family members. Online learning programmes provided by most universities are among the learning agencies where students consult the programmes for knowledge at their own pace.

Partner – Student and supervisors

Physical Learning Environment – Refers to learning in a natural setting where both learners and teachers meet physically in a physical setting. In this book, a classroom, laboratory, seminar, or workshop room is natural for students and learning agencies to interact physically.

Practices – Are norms or cultures of performing activities practically at universities that distinguish HE and other levels of education that differentiate one university from the others, such as learning and supervision quality, the acquisition of some skills, degrees, learning cultures, and the quality of graduates.

Psychosocial Learning Environment – Refers to the interactions, communications, culture, social and psychological individual and group interaction, and relationship. Psychosocial includes how the learning materials and aids are shared, organized, and communicated in HE learning environment and how the learning materials facilitate the learning process. These interactions, communication, and relationships focus mainly on the students, supervisors, leadership, and the other learning agencies.

Stakeholder – Is a generic term for all legitimated parties who influence and support HE students' learning process academically, socially, politically, and financially. These include the institutions, departments, discipline, university coordinators, students, parents/guardians, supervisors, employers, governments, and funding agencies.

Skill – The ability to perform a task well within a given time by applying specific or general expertise knowledge.

Supervision – Is an act of directing, leading, overseeing, and managing students' efforts toward agreeable learning goals. The process includes carrying out leadership roles and managerial tasks such as planning, organising, and coordinating students' efforts towards learning goals while regulating and monitoring the practices and evaluating the outcomes.

Supervisor – Is a university teacher who guides the research students through teaching and supervision. The faculty also has responsibilities to guide students' learning and ensure the implementation of institutional and governmental learning policies as a bind between the students and the institution where she is expected to perform various supervision tasks.

Structure – The arrangement of the university degrees in terms of departments, discipline, interdisciplinary, digital, and physical learning programmes, including students' supervision, assessment, and completion time arrangements.

Teacher – Refers to a university teaching staff and is used interchangeably with supervisor, academics, faculty, instructor, mentor, and a person responsible for supervising HE research students in collaboration with other learning agencies.

Abbreviations

HE	Higher Education
HEIs	Higher Education Institutions
OECD	Organisation for Economic Cooperation and Development
Ph.D.	Doctor of Philosophy (doctorate, doctoral degree)
UK	United Kingdom
USA	United States of America

List of Figures

List of Charts

Note

You may be attracted to equip yourself with more information about higher education by reading the following two books, thus, the cultural qualities you must acquire to succeed in higher education.

THE CULTURAL QUALITIES
YOU MUST ACQUIRE
TO SUCCEED IN

HIGHER EDUCATION

ELIZABETH PARADISO URASSA

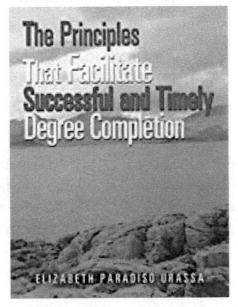

The Principles
That Facilitate
Successful and Timely
Degree Completion

ELIZABETH PARADISO URASSA

Introduction

Increasingly, most people join higher education (HE) today than in the past three decades. However, the majority lacks vital information about HE learning structure and practices that could support them prepare, adjust, and attain their degrees. People are also not aware of the changes that have occurred in HE from the 1800s to date. Others are not even aware of the knowledge and skills they desire to acquire. As a result, they enrol in HE blindly, and after sometimes they discover the situation is challenging and demanding more than their preparation and expectations. The state of blindness tends to take away the motivation needed for learning and often may end up with students dropping out. Indeed, the absence of vital information about HE is believed to be among the challenges HEIs face today, leading to students' attrition.

Short but relevant and valuable information can change people's decisions and lives. The majority can agree with me that "information is power," and its power can surpass that of many explosive weapons one can think of. The power of information may also be compared to the power of oxygen needed by all living things and all burning objects. For example, the effects of the lack of oxygen in the human body, for some minutes, may lead to lifelessness so do the burning objects. This effect can be compared to joining a university when lacking vital information about HE, leading to a degree's death. Indeed, the absence of information is the beginning of failure, which should not be embraced by people who are serious about investing in education. Little information can typically support one in making wise decisions; about why to join HE, what to learn, why now, and how to learn and acquire the knowledge and skills that will benefit society. When information about HE practices, changes, and challenges is unknown to the stakeholders, it surely leads to someone's degree's death.

Through my conversation with many people, I realised a need for a book to inform people about HE structure and practices in general. The information can change from time to time, but at least one should consider the vital mentioned aspects before and soon after joining HE. Currently, the majority do not understand the information required, and they do not think they lack information because they are not aware of what is important. Therefore, the book informs that people need to know the structure and practices of HE learning and what it takes to be a successful student. Besides, most of those who commence HE without useful information believe that learning in HE is free from challenges that students encounter in the lower levels of education. When individuals understand what's required of them and what they should expect, it may lead to adequate preparation, formulation of realistic strategies, and attaining their learning goals.

Apart from changes and challenges, there are learning contents and demands institutions pose to the students. For example, there is a limited time for completing the study, rules to be followed, and regulations to be observed in learning. Thus, students are required to adjust to individual and multicultural, and multidisciplinary learning environments. Besides, students must have acquired the appropriate personal attributes and characteristics to cooperate with various learning agencies and stakeholders. Even though some students are regarded as resourceful to their discipline, department, or even the institution, they still might have to learn from others and adjust to fit in the HE individual and collaborative learning environments. It might do with their social life about academic needs, such as positive attitudes toward their fellow students and supervisors. These demands may seem burdensome for some students who had no adequate information and preparation.

Although HE seems to be accessible to many people today, it suffers from student attrition. Some students, especially those who lack good preparation and information about the structure and practices of HE, withdraw before attaining their degrees. The weights of the diverse demands, lack of experiences in challenges, and the lack of vital information that could support students in preparation tend to be among the reasons students drop out.

I have discussed the problem of student attrition in other books, which are coming soon, thus, "The skills required of research students in supervision," and "Articulating students' expectations of competent supervisor, and the call for inspection unit for research students' supervision." In these two books, I explained some other reasons scholars indicate as the reasons for students' attrition. Indeed, several reasons cause students to drop from higher education, and that the problem call for strategies and information from all directions.

Therefore, this book will deal with information because one cannot succeed in HE learning without valid and reliable information. Though some students are encouraged or forced by some external factors (peer, family, donors, social, and economic circumstances) and the governmental police to complete their studies within a specific time, their little information about learning in HE, with unexpected demands, and unrealistic expectations, leaves a lifelong bitter mark. So, conveying right, relevant, and essential information about the HE situation can minimise and eradicate the challenges many students and other HE stakeholders are experiencing. Applicants' and Students' understanding of what is ahead of, and expected of them, can minimise the surprises, struggles, and disappointments that most of them encounter today. Having information in advance can direct and guide students and reduce students' anxiety, challenges, and attrition. Therefore, conveying correct, practical, and relevant information concerning practices and challenges in HE is what this book desires to accomplish.

People need not just information, but a trustworthy one. Unfortunately, today, the world is bombarded with much unreliable information. Therefore, scrutinising the information provided by any source is vital before applying it in decision-making or solving a problem. The information in this book comes from the scholarly literature, from the conversational interview with forty-six people with various positions and responsibilities in HEIs and with diverse backgrounds and experiences. I had unstructured conversational interviews with nine HE teachers, five dropouts HE students, eleven HE students, five-course coordinators, and three-course facilitators. Others were three donor agency representatives, six successful graduates, and four employees from diverse work backgrounds.

Information in this book observes the confidentiality and anonymity of the participants. I am sharing the information obtained from the mentioned groups according to their permission, and I respect their limits based on the kind of information to share. Besides, the informants' identities remain anonymous, and some of the information they provided has been altered without changing the meaning to cover further the identity of the informants and the institutions they operate to remain confidential. Likewise, the intertwining of names and stories has been applied to ensure that participants' identities will not be recognised by their peers, universities, or any other organ. If any story and name resemble the real story of anyone with the same name or institution, it is a coincidence, and I apologize for that.

The targeted groups for this book are people who desire to join HE and those who lack vital information on the HE learning practices. Likewise, people who are unsure which university to join and what aspects to look at when selecting a university might find the book helpful. Moreover, individuals who desire to be aware of the learning practices and the skills acquired in HE and the state of graduates' employment can benefit from reading the book. Another group is parents and guardians, who long for their children to join higher education; they may find the valuable information for advising purposes. Again, spouses may find reading the helpful book to support or discourage their partners who desire to join HE because they will understand the risks and sacrifices of their choices. I provided some experiences related to family and the issues to consider before engaging in HE learning. Other beneficiaries of this book are officials dealing with guidance and counselling of students at universities and other learning organizations. The information can also be vital for employers, financial agencies, and HE stakeholders who desire to utilize graduates' skills.

However, critical thinking is needed when dealing with any kind of information. This book is not exceptional; you must be critical and open-minded to benefit from this writing as a reader. Some information may create questions where one might desire more clarifications, advice, and references, and that discussing with others who have read the book can help clear ambiguities. It is good to share and discuss the information rather than read robotically without critical thinking and debate. Therefore, as a reader, you can also decide to utilise your time wisely by using a table of contents and select the area of your interest, even though my advice is to read the whole book. Pick what works best for you and leave everything else aside for others you know how you learn and when you learn effectively. We will always have different opinions on almost everything associated with HE learning, practices, changes, and challenges, but respecting each institution's structure and practice while reflecting and adjusting our thoughts and routines is vital. So, you are required to apply such a beautiful attribute when dealing with universities, this book, and other matters related to HE.

Therefore, this book intends to support positive preparation for HE learning. The book is not intended to discourage people who desire to join HE or display a negative portrait of HE. Rather, it recognises the position and uniqueness of

HE knowledge and the benefits it brings to individuals and societies. Although the book discloses the changes and challenges HE stakeholders encounter, it also provides some advice that may be useful to the readers and HE investors to consider. It does not intend to alter the way people think about HE learning, its position, and its vital task of producing skilled labour. The book is against dictating peoples' decisions about studying in HE and respects individual freedom of choice. Moreover, it desires to inform the readers about HE and what is needed to succeed. Therefore, if the book's ideas contradict stakeholders' perceptions on HE structure and practices and bring a debate between and among the readers, it will have served the intended goal.

Nevertheless, the structure of this book follows the arrangement in the table of contents. First, I discussed different reasons that accelerate people's desire for a degree and the experiences with learning and acquiring a degree. After that, I explained the practices of HE in the traditional era (old days before the 20 century) and the changes that have occurred leading to the modern era of HE. The writing indicates the groups that are most affected by the changes from traditional to modern HE. To explain the changes, I have applied diverse theories of learning in HE that I believe can support one to recognise the learned person. I also pointed out the learning contents and described how students learn in HE.

Furthermore, I briefly mention two types of learning contexts; physical and digital learning, where both can apply individual or collaborative learning styles. Finally, I discussed challenges HE stakeholders encounter, such as gender inequality, diverse evaluation practices, and bullying acts. To simplify the understanding of the material in each chapter, I construct some figures where each chapter consists of one figure as a summary of the discussion followed by some self-reflection questions. Also, I provide one figure that demonstrates the tasks expected of a supervisor, which demonstrates a supervisor as a "Superman." Finally, a brief conclusion is provided, followed by appendices and a list of references that have been the sources of information and can support the readers with a deeper understanding of current HE practices, changes, and challenges.

I am happy you choose to read this book; keep reading.

Chapter I
Awareness to The Reader

Most people are unaware of what is going on in HE even though they encourage their loved ones to join universities. Understanding the operation of HE might bring insight into what it takes to be a student and how to support those in universities. Indeed, several scholarly literatures inform continuous changes in HE policy, learning environments, and governmental a utonomy over institutions. Such practices are vital to comprehend before dealing with universities to make relevant and essential choices. Students and other HE stakeholders have demonstrated different perspectives about these changes, and some indicate their surprises. Therefore, I believe it is vital for HE applicants to be aware of some issues before committing to their studies. In my view, understanding the structure, challenges, and practices in HE may save many resources and may hinder students' delay in completing their degrees and attrition.

The book attempts to convey the current state of HE in many regions. It also indicates the changes in practices, demands, and necessities that call for personal transformation and an open-minded spirit. For example, the individuals' resources, values, and cultural requirements are the core aspects of the discussion in this section. Indeed, individuals ought to observe and investigate the requirements to align with their needs and consistently endure the institutional demands to meet their learning goals.

Currently, there is a vast opportunity to undertake higher education. Individuals can choose where to study and what to study to meet their learning needs if they know them. However, this can be a challenge if the persons lack vital information about HE practices and the institution, department, and discipline they desire to study. Besides, learning practices in HE is diverse, and there is no uniformity of anything, regardless of universities, regions, and continents. Most institutions, departments, and disciplines may operate differently from neighbouring, which can be challenging for some folks. Therefore, individuals who desire to join HE must identify vital services available and accessible to meet their learning needs.

Although every HEI awards several types of degrees, the individual applicant must have preferences. To understand whether the institution will meet your need, you must understand different available practices in different institutions. The ability to find the right institution with qualities that meet your needs is vital and should be observed from the beginning. Some institutions are known to produce qualitative graduates who are absorbed in the job market right after graduation. While some institutions are known for fewer quality degrees and their graduates suffer in the job market. Therefore, the applicants ought to make a wise decision during the selection of institutions, but they can do that if they understand what to look at.

Moreover, individualism must be the focus when undertaking a degree. Most people talk about collectivism and cooperation that is needed in the learning and job market today. However, not every decision or duty must operate under a collective perspective because people have different needs. Besides, in working with others, one needs to know himself very well; otherwise, others can overshadow his preferences. So, although observing others' perceptions and needs is paramount in today's cooperative world, I strongly think one needs to be himself first. For example, people around you can support you in adjusting and acquiring what you have already identified. Indeed, in the learning environment, the support to students' adjustment or learning happens if students recognize their strengths and weaknesses. Most of the time, people who cooperate with others constructively are good at self-observation and understand themselves and their needs. Therefore, the most important principle for university desiring folks is understanding what they want, need, and requirements before applying for a degree.

Self-awareness is the key to all success in HE learning. For instance, an individual needs to understand himself and the resources he possesses for learning before enrolment. Knowing "the self" may support one to understand others and what resources and characteristics are required of him. Not knowing the self from the beginning is the major weakness most students display, leading to failure to attain their learning goals. In most cases, a lack of self-understanding, self-management, and self-control results in a lack of self-discipline required in the HE learning process. Unfortunately, most individuals are neither aware of self nor the requirements and resources to accomplish their learning goals. Therefore, this book will be the first to support HE stakeholders to reflect on themselves and examine their needs with HE learning demands.

Undeniably, most individuals are joining HE with many assumptions. They are not cognisant of what is required to succeed in their learning. Besides, less has been written concerning the preparation required of individuals for HE learning to attain their education goals. Some academics have written about HE students' learning and supervision (Wisker (2005, 2012), Wisker, Kiley, & Masika (2016)), but the message favors students who have already enrolled and might not be equally valuable for individuals preparing for HE enrolment. Similarly, the writers assume HE students are mature and can comprehend the scholarly academic language and what is written about HE learning. Contrary, few students comprehend scholarly literature and that they care less about preparation for a degree. Therefore, most scholarly writings provide less information required for an individual's preparation for HE degrees.

Literature indicates that many students have commenced HE without attaining their goals (McMillan, 2005). Several students drop out due to, among others, unexpected demands associated with HE learning that they were not prepared for or willing to offer. In some countries, attrition in HE is almost 40-50%, especially for postgraduate students (Devos, Boudrenghien, Van der Linden, Azzi, Frenay, Galand & Klein (2017), Golde (2000), Laufer & Gorup (2019)). Scholarly literature has provided some reasons for student attrition, such as excessive working and family responsibilities. However, based on the conversation with my informants, I believe that some students who drop out might have lacked vital information about what it takes to be a student in HE. I also agree with the literature that jobs and family responsibilities are part of the challenge and other reasons students drop out.

Therefore, this book intends to provide vital and general information to support individuals eager to join HE or enrolled for a bachelor, master, and doctoral degree. It will sustenance them to better reflect on their decision and comprehend their needs and prepare for their studies in many areas. In addition, the book will inform HE stakeholders of some experiences people have had in HE that can support them to evaluate their desire and readiness for a degree. Individuals must scrutinise whether the knowledge and skills they intend to acquire are essential for employment. Indeed, there are differences between the knowledge and skills desired by some individuals and those needed for employment. The difference is whether the persons require knowledge for a work or job where the work is what one is talented to do and need HE to develop it no matter the monetary benefits and job is for income. Individuals ought to further investigate whether the institution of their interest and the discipline of their choice can fulfil their knowledge and skills desire, needs, and requirements. Again, to make a good decision, one must have adequate information about the practices, changes, and challenges. Therefore, by reading this book, you will be in the position to have the required awareness.

Confusing Academic Writing

In my library search, I have discovered no literature to guide individuals who desire to join HE adequately. Some of the available books are more philosophically oriented and typically written with fewer thoughts outside academic fields. Moreover, the academic language tends to be difficult for people who lack an understanding of scholarly work and are at the same time enthusiastic about joining HE. Indeed, academic writing is even more challenging for those who have not undertaken a research-related project. For instance, my informants who joined a university in the past few years informed me how difficult it was for them to understand the scholarly information written on universities' web pages and books. The first one, Judica, commented angrily:

"The language in many academic literatures is scholarly formulated and hardly for a normal person to understand. The authors normally assume that readers are on their level of understanding so, they do not have compassion for non-academic readers. For example, most authors refer to many other references where the readers need to read to understand what the writer intended to convey. One sentence might have three or more references that seem to interrupt the message planned to be conveyed. As a result, I have a problem understanding most of the scholarly publications."

Indeed, the literature for higher education subjects is sometimes complicated and is the first issue one should consider and prepare for. Students are required to read, and review documents a lot, so preparing and comprehending the number of pages one can read per day can estimate how many books one can read per month. Besides, the individuals must be aware of vocabularies and field language that may be different from expectations. Therefore, where possible, the person can search publications in his field and familiarize himself with readings.

Another person, Joseph, was also lamenting about literature; he contended,

"I have difficulty understanding scholarly literature even after I attended a workshop about the literature review. The most disturbing part is the references, which I must read in academic writing to supplement the writing in question. Sometimes I cannot read all the references provided, which is probably the main cause of not grasping the whole message. Even my supervisor has told me that I misunderstand some of the literature I apply in my writing. I wish scholars could refer their reader to few references, but the majority prefer many reading suggestions that no one can review, I think".

Joseph has a problem with reviewing the suggested references, and I think he is not alone. Scholarly writing may consist of enormous references, but it does not mean that the reader should read all of them, but at least those who desire more information on the topic have an opportunity to read the suggested publications. Furthermore, the provision of references is evidence of the sources of information; remember, academic writing deals mainly with facts, not fiction.

Although my informants found it difficult to be referred to other sources, that is the way most scholars secure the reliability of the information they provide. Undoubtedly, understanding the literature is a big challenge for both students and non-academics. The informants' explanations indicate that a single book or a single source of information can not suffice the need for reliable information about HE or any other field. However, in my opinion, not every line should have to refer the reader to another source (not in this book), but also I cannot dictate academics and their writing, but it is something folk who desire to join HE should practice.

Even though challenging, reading the provided references in academic writing brings more understanding of the topic at hand and expands the thinking capacity of the reader. It is a norm and culture of academics and scholarly writing to indicate the sources of his information and to support readers with references that may increase the knowledge of the phenomenon on hand. Therefore, it is unavoidable for the writer not to refer readers to other readings when references are available for the same topic or related topics. The culture of text referencing is the essential issue all who desire to join HE should have in mind and master after enrolment. Thus, academic writings mean a wide range of reading, the combination of materials for better understanding, and the provision of evidence to demonstrate the reliability of the information.

Nevertheless, the academics affiliated with HE institutions might encounter challenges writing the actual situation in different matters. For example, students in HE encounters diverse challenges, and in some cases, institutions' managements do nothing to support students, and that no one writes about them. Therefore, most academics employed at universities may hesitate to write their experiences working in a challenging environment, fearing contracting termination. Indeed, academic writings communicate authors' thoughts, belief patterns, and concerns, and that some do not desire their employers to comprehend their state of mind. However, most of the time, when people read some writings, they understand the thought and even the writer's feelings. Indeed, some academics' thoughts may conflict with what the government and institutions desire to hear, jeopardising their employment. This reality of conflict in thoughts and practices may limit the academics to write the reality of HE learning challenges.

People write to different audiences with different purposes. For example, writing to an audience that is not academics needs a sophisticated approach and minimisation of references to refer to. Based on my informant's description and others whom I interacted with, it seems that some who are not academics prefer adequate, reliable, and understandable information with fewer references. Indeed, it might be difficult for this group to perceive and comprehend the information conveyed by most academics in the literature. On the other hand, most information about HE is written by academics who follow the rules required in academic writing that sometimes conflict with some non-academics' thoughts. Indeed, some non-academic readers seem to misunderstand the information probably because they do not make follow up on the references provided. Therefore, exercising with academic writing and evaluate the level of understanding before joining higher education can be advantages.

On the other hand, individuals who are not part of HEIs maybe the best resource for writing helpful transformative information about HE development and challenges. For example, there is a tendency for freelances academics to be more open and with unfiltered information about some issues that can be useful for HE stakeholders to comprehend. Such openness in writing for those seeking employment in HEIs can be a stumbling block, which is why freelancers, who are not planning to work for institutions, are vital. For instance, I am a freelance writer, and I will discuss and question HE practices and write about the changes and challenges, including policies and the wellbeing of students and academics, so that HE stakeholders may understand. Their understanding may lead to positive changes that can create the best learning environment for all.

According to the principle of academic writing, I will also include text referencing in this book. Therefore, you will have an opportunity to visit other literature to connect to what I am trying to explain in some sections in this book. However, I will minimise the references as much as possible as I know the readers are not necessarily academics. Therefore, one should expect to acquire as much information as possible from this book. Although the interdependency of literature is vital, the information in this book is mainly from people who have shared their ideas, frustrations, and stories with me, and hence no need for intext references in some chapters and sections. In addition, I Have included my own experiences as a graduate from bachelor to doctoral that can also benefit the readers.

However, I could not avoid utilizing the available literature about HE, so I have consulted some academic literature to convey reliable information. Even though some references may have a different explanation from the one mentioned in this writing, I believe they will support you to understand more deeply the topic of discussion. I will always refer you to the references discussing the same topic, even though it may not favour my explanation. The aim is to expose you to diverse thoughts on the development, challenges, and practices of universities today. If you have time to read the references, you will obtain more valuable information that would either extend or criticise the book's explanations. Having diverse opinions and critical thinking are parts of the main objectives of this book.

Information Malnutrition

As I mentioned earlier, the majority do not understand what they ought to have to succeed in HE learning, and this is one of the challenges. Although most universities have conveyed information about learning opportunities and requirements on their web pages, the information does not suffice to bring the kind of understanding required by many. Likewise, the information providers (institutions) select the kind of information to share with readers. Some select information attracts students to join their institutions without providing information about the fundamental HE learning changes and challenges. As a result, knowing what it takes for an individual to be a HE student has not adequately reached the audience.

Even though students, after enrolment, consult academic advisors for information, most of the knowledge from these advisors seems to focus on the technical issues such as learning procedures, rules, and regulations that students should observe. In addition, advisors are responsible for representing the institutions and their interests as much as possible and tend to have little attention to students' needs. In some circumstances, students are forced to adjust to the institutional needs, and that demoralises them. Therefore, sometimes, academic advisors are not good advocates for students' challenges, and they might not understand, and report students' concerns the way students desire.

One of the dropout students, Lilly, asserted, *"The information some advisors share with students are filtered to fulfil the need of their employers (HEIs), and sometimes students' needs are not considered important. I struggled with one academic advisor without obtaining the support I needed. I changed the advisor, and I faced the same problem of not being heard. I felt lonely and had no one to support me. Even when I was informed about the bullying behaviour of my supervisor, no one managed to take any action. It is frustrating how academics and the institution administrators support each other without thinking of the students' situation. For this reason, I had to quit."*

The student blamed academic advisors for not cooperating and supporting her with what she observed as bullying in supervision. As a result, she felt abandoned and not heard by those expecting to obtain their support. The misunderstanding and the lack of support she was experiencing made her drop out.

Another issue to bear in mind is that most universities decide what students should hear, do, and whatnot. For example, the information provided on institutions' web pages dictates what information to provide to people and capture their perceptions. Unfortunately, the information about the institution's weaknesses and challenges students may encounter after enrolment is missing. For example, I checked many institutions' web pages, and no one had a place where they inform their weaknesses or ask applicants, in advance, what kind of expectations they have and what skills and competencies they need or desire to acquire or develop. The information on the institutions' websites is more technical and associated with the needs and requirements of the institutions.

They inform about rules, regulations, benefits, and courses provided and their duration, and all are positive with smiling faces.

For example, the information about when and where to undertake some courses, deadlines of some assignments and examinations, seminars, and workshops available online and on-campus are the information that dominates the contents of most universities' web pages. Likewise, the procedures to follow in case of complaints and changing of supervisors and other social affairs are the most preferable by some universities. Very seldom will the readers come across information about the challenges and changes of practices in HE, which can hinder students from learning. They do not mention policies that dominate their institutions and their effects on students' learning and graduation. Information about what to do to succeed in HE learning is absent even though HE stakeholders need such information.

According to my conversations with some people, I discovered that some have different information concerning HE learning. Some of the information needs modifications and others are destructive. The majority also has many unrealistic expectations about HE that are based on the traditional era of elite HE. Besides, the idea of HE learning and the position of supervisors are complicated to many HE stakeholders. I did not intend to discuss why people join universities, but I found it difficult to avoid this part of the discussion because it is vital and can support someone to re-examine his/her motive for a degree. Indeed, learning in HE is a serious project, and that knowing why people engage in such demanding tasks is vital. As a reader, you also will find this discussion about HE practices useful if you understand why people join HE and need a degree.

Although I mentioned the lack of relevant and vital information about HE learning, some people believe it might be unfair to blame HEIs for not providing adequate information about their practices. Contrary, some institutions have no adequate information about why people need a degree from their institution. In this case, considering why people desire a degree is vital in assessing the information required to provide. Therefore, universities must convey information based on the reason for people to join their institutions. The information will also support stakeholders and readers to comprehend why people need a degree or why their family members or employees need a degree. Such people may understand the criterion to observe when selecting the institution for the HE studies. However, the book has many questions unanswered as the aim is to highlight what is going on in most universities in general. It does not intend to provide details or breastfeeding anyone with information but makes the readers and stakeholders aware of issues that they may find more information about. The information in this book is a catalyst for readers to think critically and yet ask many questions. For example, the first question is, why a degree?

Chapter II
Why DO People Need A DEGREE?

It is vital to understand why people desire to acquire a degree. Several reasons make individuals of all backgrounds opt for a degree today. Diverse groups of individuals with diverse backgrounds join HE every year: single and married, male and female, young and elderly, experienced and non-experienced, aim to acquire a degree. Indeed, why people need a degree, seems complicated to answer, especially if we lack information about how HE learning is organised and the expected outcomes. No single satisfactory response can explain why people opt for a degree, especially this time, and this is to say the question may have diverse responses to as diverse people who respond to it.

Often, people learn for a purpose, and some learn not for a degree but to acquire specific knowledge and skills. Therefore, they may drop anytime they observe acquiring what they desired and not necessarily completing their degree studies. Therefore, successful learning is measured by the degree to which the learners attain the intended learning goals[1] and not always the graduation. However, it is challenging to assess individual learning objectives and believe one has attained the learning goal if he does not complete the programs intended for the degree. So, the norms of HE is to ensure that students enrolled for a degree complete their program as one step of attaining the intended learning goals. However, one must scrutinise the knowledge and skills of graduates because completing the degree programs sometimes does not indicate the acquisition of intended competencies.

Therefore, each individual needs to comprehend his learning goal before commencing HE to measure the outcomes better. Surprisingly, some students

---

[1]A goal is a desired result that an individual student plans and commits to attain in a certain period through working with a specific assignment or project.

are not aware of their learning goals neither the skills and competencies they are looking for, and some are uncertain why they should acquire a degree. Some individuals have commenced HE studies and realised later that the university, department, faculty, and even the degree they opted for could not provide them with the skills and competencies they were looking for. We have witnessed people who have taken different degrees of the same levels consecutively and still have not acquired the knowledge and skills they desire.

For example, some people have two or more bachelor's, master's, and doctoral degrees, one after the other, in the same field or different. Higher education is costly, and I do not believe one should learn in HE for fun. There are diverse reasons for repeating studying the same and similar level of a degree; among others, lack of information before commencing could make the persons set their learning goals clear and ensure the study will meet them. Without such an evaluation and clear understanding of what the study provides, individuals cannot set the learning objectives and fail to attain the expected skills. Regrettably, if the acquisition of, let us say, "parallel degrees" happen without the attainment of specific knowledge and skills or attaining the intended goals, it can be regarded as a waste of resources. Although one can argue that it is an investment and accumulation of knowledge, expertise out of use might be a burden to the owner. Learning by goals and with a specific intention might be more profitable and can be measured clearly. All learners should attain their intended learning goals, and the utility of the knowledge and skills acquired should be the principal goal rather than just accumulating them.

I asked five graduates who have parallel degrees (two had two bachelor degrees and two master degrees in education, three had two master degrees in the science field) why they decided to acquire two equivalent degrees. They demonstrated different reasons for their decisions. I shall not separate their responses either to discuss it deeply, and I shall inform you in general what their argument was. Among the reasons that led them to take the second master's degrees was the dissatisfaction of the previous master's degree and lack of specific learning goals during the first master's degree and graduated without the knowledge and skills they needed.

Two of the five graduates mentioned that employment difficulties made them study for another master's degree with high demand in the job market. Another two revealed that the availability of funding to undertake a new master's degree was so unpretentious that it motivated them to study again. One of the students admitted that he did not require a master's degree, based on his career choice, but he desired to travel to another country for exposure. She received a beautiful scholarship, which was her catalyst to study again for a master's degree. They all admitted that they enrolled in the first master's degree without clarifying what skills and knowledge to acquire and utilising their competencies.

Nevertheless, the majority have different perspectives and reasons for longing for a degree. Some focus on the advantages associated with a degree for individuals and society. Others look for the learning process advances such as scholarships, exposure, and relations, while some focus on exceptional research knowledge and skills obtained in HE. Such a diverse understanding of a degree's learning benefits is primarily grounded in the historical background of HE, its functionalities, and its advantages. However, I shall take the risk to suggest some of the reasons that have accelerated most people's desire for a degree. These reasons emanate from my conversation with informants who narrate their experiences and from literature.

Acquisition of Specific Professional Skills

Some people join HE to acquire specific knowledge and skills. The majority desires to become researchers, teachers, writers, leaders, and other professionals that demand high critical thinking capability. This desire has made many universities establish degrees even in the departments that traditionally had no degree programmes (arts and music and others). The availability of degrees in different disciplines has given people of different professions access to HE for research degrees. Besides, people can study part-time, full-time online, and in a physical setting, and that most people can integrate work and studies (Lesley Cooper, Janice Orrell, & Margaret Bowden, 2010). These groups of people who desire to develop specific knowledge and skills and enhance their professions tend to focus mainly on the expertise acquired through HE absents in lower levels of education. Likewise, some scholars have indicated the knowledge produced in HE and its peculiarity and diverse levels of awareness and duties individuals should carry to succeed.

For instance, according to Bloom's taxonomy of learning (Anderson, Krathwohl, Bloom, & Benjamin (2001), Krathwohl (2002), Weigel & Bonica (2014)), the HE may be positioned at the highest level of Bloom's taxonomy of educational hierarchy. At this level, a learner is expected to compare, judge, criticise and evaluate ideas, plans, and apply concepts to create new or better concepts. Individual critical thinking is typically expected in HE, where students evaluate the work of others through literature review and find a knowledge gap. Students in HE, especially research students, learn to fill the knowledge gaps in the field of interest. The intention is to bring new and better knowledge of the topic or the field and even solve the existing challenges. Therefore, students undergo different stages to acquire the knowledge and skills that empower them to reach the point of creating new and applicable knowledge to cover the gap (Kiyama & Rios-Aguilar, 2017). Although the process might be challenging and with several setbacks, this process results in the acquisition of diverse skills, which is the primary aim of learners.

Advancement of the Technology

Another factor facilitating enrolment in HE is the availability of information through technology. Information written on most institutions' web pages has become a catalyst for many to be aware of the different degrees offered in HEIs. Currently, almost every university, even from rural and poor regions, has its websites to display information about their services (based on what they want the applicant to believe) and how easy and beneficial it is to enroll in HE. In addition, the enrolment process has been simplified by the development of technology and, specifically, the internet, where people access information by clicking a button.

Contrary, in the early days (in the 1900s), when people communicated by letters, some got lost without reaching the intended persons or organizations. Currently, one needs to click on the right place to obtain and receive the desired information. Indeed, most universities require their applicants to apply online by sending the information required electronically in the HE application. Likewise, the responses can take a few weeks, if not instantly, or some days, and the communication, most of the time, is effective, quick, and reliable. If an individual has questions, they are answered quickly through chat, video communication, and other means. Indeed, this effective, quick, and reliable technological communication influence many to access the information and enrol in HE.

Aggressive Marketing

Another trick which traps many people to join HE is marketing strategies. Indeed, the accessibility of information about the cost of education and how easy it may be to obtain a scholarship has become a stimulus. Most universities have information about where to apply for funding and all the necessary information concerning the funding and enrolment. Although few applicants obtain such financial support, universities still apply this strategy to attract students. There are different methods universities are applying to connect with those interested in studying in their institution and even calling them and motivating them to make a quick decision. Some advisors, although not a good idea, promise some applicants of financial support. This quick and tricky information about funding and enrolment tends to increase people's curiosity, and hence some have joined HE based on this kind of misleading promise.

For instance, one of my informants, Eva, was curious about searching and reading information online about HE enrolment. She had no plan to enrol in any university at that time, but she just wanted to read and have helpful information that could help her later. The female applicant finally landed on a university's web page, and immediately the chatting box appeared. The chatting asked her whether she had any questions, and the chat introduced itself as students' advisor from the University. Indeed, she had some questions, so she communicated with the chat advisor, who managed to answer almost all the questions she had. They kept on chatting for a while, and the advisor was very welcoming and worked hard to convince her to enroll as quickly as possible due to the fee discount that would end soon. Unfortunately, this was just a trick because the discount information persisted for months after their first chat.

Deciding to join HE under pressure may be a regrettable idea. Nevertheless, Eva told the advisor that she needed to decide because she had some family and financial challenges. The advisor agreed with her, but he also indicated that it might be easier for her to obtain financial support from the university if she enrolled and paid some advanced money. The advisor ended his conversation by asking for her contact for future communication with her. Eva provided him with all the information he requested for further contact, and she was pleased with the information she received.

After two days, Eva was surprised by a call from a man who introduced himself as a student advisor from the same university. His concern was to ask whether the female had made up her mind about enrolment. She indicated the dilemma she was having and still needed sometimes and that she might not enrol due to other plans. Therefore, Eva received a call almost every week from the university bombarding her with attractive information. Finally, she enrolled with little preparation, and her decision was supported by only the marketing strategies applied by the advisor and the university web page.

Enrolling in HE with little information has several consequences. Eva enrolled, but she did not obtain financial support as the advisor suggested. Her financial situation and the family were so demanding that she had to drop her studies within the first year of her enrolment. I am writing this to make you aware that most universities have aggressive marketing strategies. This kind of marketing induces pressure and stress on individuals and might lead to a quick unprepared decision to join HE. I am convinced that the university advisors who call people around for enrolment are business-oriented and might have a low quality of educational services. It is best for individuals receiving calls from universities to carefully examine and take time to make good decisions on their own without pressure. However, this aggressive marketing is one of the factors that is believed to have increased students' enrolment in HE.

Desire to Absorb New Cultures

However, some people join higher education for cultural purposes. As I will discuss later, the learning environment of HE has changed to a multicultural environment. The students and faculties are from diverse backgrounds and are expected to meet and cooperate in diverse ways regardless of their background. This kind of interaction facilitates learning about various cultural practices, which may be beneficial in understanding other peoples' thoughts and actions. Furthermore, in considering other peoples' cultures, students are typically provided with opportunities to share their culture and exchange with others. Comprehending diverse cultures is a colossal assertion required today and maybe one of the motives for some people to desire a degree in a multicultural learning environment.

There are two primary cultures that students in HE are exposed to. The first is an independent culture where students learn to work independently on all levels of their studies. For example, students need to choose discipline, courses, and research topics independently or with little support from their supervisors and focus on their choices. Moreover, the students must demonstrate their understanding of their learning needs and requirements independently, even when they are in a group. The independent learning part of HE is demonstrated in students' assessment and certification, where a certificate is awarded to an individual graduate, not to a group. In addition, the learning system and the way learning materials and guidance are organised and provided in HE enhances independent and individual critical thinking (Goldthorpe, 2007) and decision making. Therefore, independence in learning, by observing time managing and self-discipline skills are some of the influential cultures students need to learn and master.

Secondly, the students are exposed to an interdependent learning culture where they ought to cooperate with several other learning agencies (Carter, 2014) for their successful learning. Students are encouraged to tackle some problems collectively, and such practices create a co-dependency between and among them. For example, students depend on other agencies than supervisors for well and safe accommodation. Having a safe and comfortable accommodation facilitate students with the concentration required on their studies. Lack of reliable, affordable, and comfortable accommodation may lead to a lack of focus on the studies, and hence the accommodation manager is as essential as faculty. Besides, students need not only housing but other facilities such as learning materials. So, in most universities, a facility manager who ensures students' study space and other learning materials such as computers, chairs, and tables is part of students' learning agencies, and students depend on these persons for learning. These kinds of interactions with diverse people and learning agencies enhances interdependent culture.

Interdependency between students and learning agencies enhances the learning of diverse cultures. For example, in my master's degree learning, a student could not use some facilities because of health issues. She sent a request to the facility manager asking for better equipment to cater to her learning needs. The manager had to order the required tools for the student. While waiting for the items, the student could not concentrate on her studies and had to wait for more than two weeks to receive the relevant facilities. All this time, she was restless and could not be able to follow the learning. Indeed, it indicates the importance of facility managers and other learning agencies to students even though academic services sometimes shadow their duties.

At the same time, the students need to understand how to express their needs appropriately to the right people. They must have self-direction of how to go about and demonstrate their need correctly, and in this process, they learn and interact with new communication cultures. The facility manager, for example, is one of the many learning agencies that students in HE depend on for learning. These learning agencies have diverse backgrounds and cultures that students must observe to obtain the service they require. Therefore, learning in HE facilitates autonomous and symbiotic cultures that may motivate some people to join HEIs.

Desire to Share the Experiences

Moreover, another factor accelerating HE enrolment these days is the ambition to share experiences. Some matured students have life experiences connected to the diverse field of studies that have allowed them to see differences between scientific knowledge and non-scientific knowledge in real life (Manathunga, Lant, & Mellick, 2007). They have probably implemented both non-scientific and scientific ideas stipulated by their leaders, governments, and other actors through jobs or other life responsibilities. They have had different roles, and they understand the consequences of implementing both (scientific and unscientific) knowledge sources (Crebert, Bates, Bell, Patrick, & Cragnolini (2004), Eustace, Baird, Saito, & Creedy (2016), Powell (2013)). Their experiences might have made them have knowledge that might be beneficial to the field they are interested in, and they have ambitions to contribute to making a difference. Therefore, for their dream to come true, they join HE as a platform to display what they know and share their experiences.

For instance, one doctoral degree student informed me that her desire to share her experiences was the catalyst for joining a doctorate study. The female student had worked as a job advisor for more than twenty years before commencing the doctoral degree, and she had observed the mistake some advisors conducted when advising job seekers. She researched to find out what do advisors need to inform job seekers and why? The student had some hypotheses based on her experience as a job advisor and the practices of other advisors. According to her experience, the advisors who promised their clients the support to find a job created a thought that the advisor could find them a job without their active engagement. At the same time, the advisor who asks clients about their plans and strategies to find jobs, made their clients more active and thriving. The former job advisor shared her experiences and conducted research that proves that her hypotheses were valid because sometimes people need more questions than advice. Therefore, some people's experiences and hypotheses are the interest that they desire to test and share through HE learning.

Demand for Research Knowledge

Apart from the mentioned reasons, another factor accelerating HE enrolment is the increasing demands on research knowledge. The world has come closer and sharing of information needs a close investigation to understand its reliability. Individuals, industries, businesses, and organisations are keen to hire critical thinking people who solve problems scientifically (Lee (2007), Park (2007)). For example, most businesses collapse if their owners do not research the areas they must maintain their investment and the areas that need modification. It might be difficult for anyone to prosper in business without researching the vital aspects such as customers' preferences. Even the small businesses, who have no formal education, without researching their products and customers' satisfaction, cannot survive.

For example, I realised recently that village bread sellers have a lot of research information about their customers' preferences. I am fond of a flatbread called *"chapati,"* and I often buy it from different shops and restaurants. However, I bought a flatbread that tested differently from the others from a particular village in a new region. The bread was very soft, smelled good, and very delicious with a unique taste. I had to go back to the shopkeeper the following day and asked, what was the secret behind the excellent taste of the bread? She hesitated to tell me her secret and told me I could apply and take her customers if I knew the secret. Therefore, I had to ensure her that I was not asking for doing business or sharing the information, but my curiosity.

She reluctantly told me the secret by saying: *"I always mix the wheat flour with something else* (she mentioned the staff) *that other bakers do not apply."* I asked her whether she had had feedback from other customers about the superb taste of her bread? She replied: *"Yes, of course, I made an investigation and found that most customers like the taste and smell of my bread now than before, and that is why I keep on using the same ingredient."* She added that from the time she applied the ingredient, she had tripled the customers. She also informed that she was still learning how to attract more customers and probably will increase the size of the bread to be bigger than other sellers.

In fact, "the flatbread lady" was a good researcher because I also liked the taste of the bread, and all the times I was in that region, I had to drive a distance away to buy the bread from her. It was part of her scientific investigation that led her to sell the bread more than other sellers. The beautiful issue with researching change and development is that it never ends; one needs to study day after day for new knowledge.

Indeed, in the chaos of the market-driven economy, several cases that indicate the necessity of research knowledge. For example, changes in products such as cell phones, computers, and other electronic products occur very quickly these days based on consumer research-based information. To meet consumers' demands, the companies typically ask for the users' feedback about the products, and their suggestions are vital to develop or alter the business. The companies find out what customers typically complain about, and they solve the problems with a new product that caters to the purpose. This kind of investigation and feedback provides scientific information for the companies to modify the products, manufacture new products, and even maintain the product. The information from consumers is what we refer to as research-based information. Therefore, research-based knowledge is highly needed to fulfil peoples' demands and sometimes may change people's beliefs, thoughts, and actions.

Undoubtedly, research knowledge is vital and needed by every person. Every individual requires to act as a professional researcher, especially in today's world of controversial information. The flood of digital information through different channels needs critical thinking to filter the correct, from incorrect, fake from accurate, constructive from destructive one. It might be not only the challenge of fake news, which can be destructive, but the concepts created in the mind of readers who have no critical thinking can be even more damaging. People need to have the ability to differentiate facts and opinions and to read, write and spread constructive information critically. It threatens the way people consider and confuse opinion, facts, and speculation due to a lack of research skills. Therefore, research knowledge is essential no matter what problem one is dealing with today and is highly needed.

Understandably, not all knowledge comes from research findings. All knowledge should not necessarily emanate from research because some knowledge originates from intuitive and spiritual experiences. Sometimes, people experience something as a revelation of its existence that science cannot explain. Indeed, spiritual, and unexplainable information has been supportive to people for ages, and most of the knowledge from such intuitive has been beneficial to the majority, as explained by Bone (2007), Chatterjee & Krishnan (2007). However, even for issues that lack explanation, people need to be curious about finding its reality, hence research. Generally, all information should be scrutinised scientifically and critically for its reliability, no matter its source. Even the knowledge claimed originated from supernatural power need scrutinization to avoid deceptions.

Conducting research is not a new phenomenon neither something complicated. Scrutinising, criticising, doubting, and finding more information about issues has been with humans for ages. It started in the garden of Eden when Adam was told not to eat the fruit from the tree of good and evil. I believe he informed his wife, Eve, a researcher, and she began researching by asking one informant, Satan. She had two hypotheses in her research where one support the notion that if they ate the fruits, they had to die as their master told them, and another hypothesis was the opposite. The research results indicated that the notion was true, and they died instantly spiritually and gradually physically. Therefore, research is not a new phenomenon but old philosophy that supports humans to find the reality of information and solutions to problems.

Indeed, most organisations' development and success depend on how quickly they can find and apply research information[2] to their daily activities. Whether it is service provider organisations, products producers, or policymakers, the need to research for the betterment of their provision, productions, and decisions is vital. So, research-based knowledge is required in all areas of human life, which has increased the demand for HE learning.

Laboratory activities are part of scientific research but not the only way of making a scientific investigation. Formally, people thought scientific knowledge should come only from laboratory and mathematically calculated items with a specific measurement and statistical demonstration through quantitative research method (Creswell, Plano Clark, Gutmann & Hanson (2003), Creswell (2018). Currently, the majority acknowledges that scientific knowledge might come from stories and peoples' experiences without experiments and mathematics. The kind of information people collect through conversation is among the scientific information from the qualitative research method. Conversation and narrative storytelling are among the qualitative research designs people apply to collect scientific information (Creswell (2018), Johnson & Christensen (2008), Onwuegbuzie, Frels, Leech, & Collins (2011). The information emanates from the interaction with people through purposive interviews, focus group

---

[2] Information obtained from reliable sources scrutinised critically and analyses interpreted according to the intention required.

discussions about specific issues they are familiar with; this conversation can be led by pre-prepared questions or an unstructured conversation using open-ended questions.

Likewise, to be successful in all areas of our lives today, we need to do some research to gain reliable and helpful information about what we desire to understand. Even if we need a partner, we must research his background, hobbies, and lifestyle. It bothers me to see many people joining HE without researching its services, practices, and challenges. I believe that reading this book is evidence that you are doing good research about HE, and if you want to be more knowledgeable and successful, you need to read all chapters of this book. Therefore, you are researching to discover more about HE and whether it is an excellent decision to acquire a degree. If you have enrolled already, you might have read this book to learn how to adjust and work with other learning agencies smoothly and successfully. All in all, you are doing research no matter what you intend to do with this reading. You have made an excellent decision to choose this book for research.

It is not the intention of this book to discuss research methods, but you can read the references by Creswell (2015, 2007, 2018), Creswell & Plano Clark (2011) about research methods of different kinds. However, researching every issue in our lives and collecting information even without an experiment and statistics method is vital. Undeniably, the daily research demand has forced people to join HE to acquire professional research skills.

Economic Benefits for the Individual and Society

Likewise, the economic benefits associated with HE is another motive for many to opt for HE. Although some people desire to minimize the power of formal education, it is believed that the more educated an individual becomes, the more he benefits from the societal resources. In this case, the majority support the human capital theory of investing in the human mind through education for future benefits (Madan (2018), Sweetland (1996), Throsby (1999)). This philosophy is not for those who focus on quick earning but those who desire to integrate well-rounded knowledge and skills. We have also seen that societies with HE graduates benefit from the individuals' knowledge and skills than without, hence the development (Simpson, 1983). The trend of the relationship between education and human development is explained by Simpson, who informed on how HE graduates challenged unscientific political decisions in

Germany. He also demonstrated how graduates contributed to their society with scientific knowledge that led to social-economic development. Therefore, without doubt, HE knowledge empowers people and facilitates their ability to question decision-makers and implementers in their conduct. Furthermore, the love of scientific knowledge motivates most governments to engage in HE issues and support HEIs (Stensaker, Frolich, Gornitzka, & Maassen, 2008).

In addition, the personal gain from education has been a motive for people to enroll in HE learning. For example, Bourdieu (1990) discussed the various capital that a person and society can obtain through education. First, HE increases economic capital for the graduates as compared to other levels of education. Second, the learning content improves individuals' knowledge value, and that the graduates are assumed to have acquired knowledge and skills that legitimate them to occupy decision-making positions. Third, locally and globally, graduates tend to have high monetary and social status benefits that are sources of other forms of capital.

According to Tholen (2014):

"The OECD stresses that; human capital accumulation is an important determinant of individuals' earning capacity and employment prospects, and therefore plays an important role in determining the level and distribution of income." (p. 3).

Again, even if the individuals do not occupy decision-making positions, the skills expected of graduates and the networks created during their learning may lead to personal and social capital accumulation that may open other privileges. The network and the knowledge, skills, and competencies that graduates possess may facilitate their effective functioning in the job market locally and globally. Their network tends to strengthen their performance and increase social capital that often creates other capitals. The network graduates have may be different from the one people describe in social media and other platforms.

Moreover, some graduates obtain symbolic capital (Bourdieu (1990), Neveu (2018)) through their work. For example, in an academic environment, there are scholars whose work is vital in specific fields, and often time these scholars are honoured for their work through referencing and citations. Their contributions are vital, qualitative, and worthy of being pursued and preserved in the field they play and beyond. They do not choose themselves to be honoured, but it is the judgment of others who have evaluated their work and place them in an advantageous position. Recognition is a kind of honour that results in the quality work of an individual and is embodied to that person as capital and, most of the time, cannot be transferred to someone else.

According to the explanation of capital provided by Bourdieu (1990), one may conclude that HE is among the tools that facilitate the accumulation of capital that reside in the individual. I am convinced that HE can provide different capitals simultaneously, thus, economic, cultural, social, and symbolic capital (to mention a few). His information might have inspired those who have read Bourdieu's ideas of capital. The information from scholarly literature about the economic benefits of HE can be one of the catalysts that motivate some people to join HE.

Besides, several dialogues unfold the benefits associated with a degree. Most of the time, motivational speakers from several social mediums (see appendix 2) disclose personal satisfaction with acquiring a degree. They usually reflect on the usefulness of individuals' knowledge and how the knowledge changes identity. Graduates become part of the educated class and, of course, the knowledge acquired legitimises them to solve challenges facing societies scientifically (Hall & Burns (2009), McAlpine (2012)). If we refer to Simpson (1983), the graduate's identity changes upon graduation from ordinary civilian to professional or skilled labour. He lectured farmers and convinced the investors to invest in a chemical factory for agriculture based on his research findings. Therefore, people with identity have more opportunities to utilize and share their knowledge and skills to benefit others. Acquiring social capital is one of many reasons which has motivated people to join HE.

Family and Individual Status

Family is another institution that motivates people to join HE. Most family members believe that education can change their members' lives and the lives of their loved ones for the better. Besides, some families think that education changes their position and increases their status in society and that the more educated an individual is, the more responsible he becomes in society. For example, today, parents and guardians are working hard to support their children for HE in their countries or abroad. To the majority, HE has become the cornerstone for recognition, acquisition of networks, new cultures, and new people in their lives. Some families also desire their members to acquire HE abroad to visit them and experience different cultures (Usher (2002), Wisker,

46

Robinson, Trafford, Lilly, & Warnes (2004)). There is a belief that the whole family will benefit from the educational outcomes upon successful individual graduation.

The gravity from families has become a driving force for some young and older people to join HE. Sometimes, the pressure is significant to the extent of becoming a punishment, and some parents and guardians threaten to withdraw their favour from their children if the individuals do not join HE. One lady, Mariam, explained how her husband induced pressure to join HE, although they had small children. She asserted: *"I could not believe it when my husband came with the idea of studying abroad. He saw an advertisement about women's scholarships and started bothering me about taking a master's degree abroad. My younger child was two years, and the elder one was four. I wanted my children to have an education in our country, especially primary education, because they could have a good foundation of our culture, including the language. However, my husband had an agenda of working abroad to widen his engineering profession and enhance his English. There was a conflict of thoughts between my husband and me, and he won. So, I applied for the scholarship and headed for a master's degree abroad with the whole family."*

The husband to this female student desired to work abroad, and because the wife could obtain a women's scholarship, he pressurised her to study abroad. He anticipated his wife could allow him to have the opportunity to work abroad and learn the language. So, she joined HE under that kind of pressure without good preparation mentally, and much was expected from her. She went on through a lot of, what she called, stressful periods, but at last, she graduated successfully. She admitted that she would not have been able to graduate timely without pressure from her husband and other family members. However, she said, the pressure was sometimes overwhelmed, and she graduated exhaustedly and could continue with neither academic nor non-academic work. She remained the mother taking care of her two beautiful children to date, and she thinks she has not benefited from the knowledge she acquired as expected. Yes, pressure from family members has forced many to join HE even without preparation, where some have become successful, and others not. However, families contribute to the increased enrolment in most universities.

Infrastructure Advancement

Moreover, the advanced infrastructure facilitates mobility and accessibility of most prestigious foreign institutions (Blumenthal (1996), Marginson & van der Wende (2009)). However, most third-world countries have few universities compared to the successful students who need to join HE. Their institutions cannot accommodate all their qualified and enthusiastic candidates, and hence some must seek university education abroad. For example, there are scholarships for students coming from developing countries, and most students from these countries are the beneficiaries of scholarships provided worldwide (see appendix 1). However, the majority have to borrow money from banks for HE abroad. Besides, international students have access to universities worldwide based on their qualifications and requirements. The mobility could not happen if the infrastructure were poor.

Likewise, the students who study abroad have to travel from their home countries. We can think of advanced means of airplanes, ships, and other automobiles connecting different continents, regions, and districts, making it easy for people to move across borders. Even with coronavirus, still, people's movement continues in a different style. Indeed, international students are not the only ones who desire to live and study on campus, but even those who study in their countries, some opt to conduct research abroad. Currently, students can research in their home country while enrolled in a foreign university or vice versa. Indeed, infrastructure advancement has made it possible for students to move from one region to another. People can research or enrol in any institution in the world where they are qualified, and hence easy access to HE.

Similarly, students from western countries have some exchange programmes that allow students to study abroad for some time. For example, there are students from Europe going to South Africa, Tanzania, and other African countries for a semester or two for specific courses. In addition, some students are heading to Asia, South America, and other parts of the world where they can study or conduct researchers for a certain period. The exchange program internationally is possible due to, among others, the advancement of the infrastructure, including transport and accommodation. Students can search online and find different offers related to transport and accommodation and make choices depending on their financial ability. Therefore, the development has increased accessibility and might incentivize people to desire a degree.

Peer Pressure

Other people join HE studies due to peer pressure. Some individuals observe being left behind by their peers if they do not join, HE. For example, one young man was employed as a salesman in a particular company. Although he liked his job, he was not able to settle and work because all his friends had joined HE abroad. The worse thing is that they often sent him photos showing their enjoyment in the new learning environment, which was devastating. Besides, he was academically (according to the summative grades) the brightest of all other friends in the bachelor's degree. His ego could not let him work joyfully anymore, and he thought he had made the mistake of not opting for a master's degree as his peers. Therefore, he started losing interest in his job and searched for a master's degree position, and finally joined one university.

There is nothing worse than joining HE due to external pressure. The salesman had no idea what skills he wanted to acquire to be more productive than he was in the job. His employer did not support his idea because he was a productive, active, and qualified employee. Therefore, the young man did not receive financial support for his master's degree studies. Likewise, the salesman could not convince his employer of the company's benefits from his master's degree nor inform the skills and competencies he will acquire.

Nevertheless, the man desired to cope with friends, so he asked for study permission without payments to pursue the intended master's degree. Indeed, it was tough because he did not receive financial support from his employer either a scholarship. Therefore, he headed to a bank to borrow some money for his studies, creating economic hardship. Unfortunately, while studying, something happened with his employers' company, and his position was no longer needed. After graduation, he had no job to return to, and it took him sometimes to get a well-paid job like the one he had before. He admitted to me that some colleagues have a lower level of education and have a higher financial benefit than himself in the new job. Without a doubt, the young man was disappointed because he had increased financial debt simply because of comparing himself with peers. In addition, he realized later that he did not need a degree but was grateful for the knowledge and skills from HE.

Indeed, the story of the young man is a reminder that not all people need a degree. Even if we talk about social and financial benefits associated with a degree, it should not be the motive. However, some people are exposed to pressure from their peers and join HE without critical consideration. However, I reminded him that the satisfaction he has obtained after acquiring a degree may supers the financial gain and should be one of the positive results to focus on. Certainly, HE and a degree cannot be measured in monetary benefit only, but other aspects such as a new identity and personal satisfaction play a part. Yes, peer pressure may accelerate the enrolment in HE today.

The Availability of Finances

The other reason may be the availability of financial resources. Currently, there are several sources of funds that an individual may utilise, such as donor agencies, bank loans, and governments support. These funds have increased in the last three decades, and they are reliable for HE learning. Indeed, HE's funding system has made children of less privileged families access education and become skilled laborers. Therefore, the funding sources can be a motivating agent for increasing people longing for a degree.

For example, several reliable donor agencies are looking for motivated and qualified people to undertake a research degree. In addition, there are several scholarships advertisements in different universities and other organizations' web pages for people to apply. See Appendix 1 in this book, where I indicate a list of donor agencies listed at 2021/2022 for scholarships (Take it just as an example because the information about scholarships changes often). These donors indicate the number of funds and the conditions to meet to get financial support. Hence, those who desire to join HE and looking for financial support may be interested to review the web pages provided in the appendix.

Fairness is one of the qualities most donor agencies observe. Besides, no one needs to know someone or have a godfather in advance to get a scholarship. Reliable donor agencies explain the applicants' requirements and whoever fulfils the requirements is eligible for the scholarship. However, not all qualified can obtain the scholarship, and the choice depends on the funds available and the number of candidates the donor intends to support. The conditions stipulated by donor agencies vary with their interests and the nature of the scholarship. I cannot emphasize enough how important it is for the individual to read carefully and understand the information provided by the donor agencies before sending an application. It might be beneficial to check whether the organisation you intend to apply for funds has interests that match yours. Some donor agencies' interests may be different from yours and may jeopardise your freedom of future career.

Therefore, as an applicant, one must be observant and apply for funds to reliable donor agencies and organisations that correspond to your interest.

Typically, scholarships have different features one should comprehend. Sometimes, the scholarships may cover all or some learning expenses, and the applicant must observe from the beginning. Similarly, the scholarship does not always mean relaxing and enjoying your studies because some donors can decide to finance only part of the costs and create a kind of cost-sharing policy with you. Therefore, the students should pay some costs by either working part-time or finding another donor or source of finance for the rest of the uncovered costs. Scrutinising the scholarship advertisements closely and understand the scope and limits the bursary poses at the very beginning. You can read the information provided in the list of donor agencies in appendix 1 as an example to learn how different their conditions and offers can be. Familiarizing with some donor countries and organizations and their demands can save much time applying to resolve disputes.

Donor agency requirements can sometimes be overwhelming. The conditions vary from one donor to another, and even what they need in return varies. Sometimes most donors need knowledge of something and hence provide the area of studies that one should engage in. Others do not have a specific area of study, rather a specific group of individuals or demographics they desire to support. However, most of them are interested in something or some people of a particular group (minority, female, girls, boys, male) or field.

Moreover, donors look for more reliable and capable candidates who are motivated and can demonstrate the ability to complete the studies within a specific time. For example, the scholarship might focus on females from developing countries, leadership positions, or other criteria. Furthermore, the scholarship agencies can demand that the project or study relate to a certain theme, coronavirus, environment, leadership, or any other topic or problem affecting people locally or globally.

Sometimes, no specific issue or subject is required, but the applicant must have acquired specific qualifications or achievements. For example, the person's ambitions should be written through the study intent where the person indicates a certain level of competencies in a particular field and how the education will strengthen the individuals' practices. Another time the donors need to understand the language of instruction or grades in specific academic subjects or discipline, and sometimes, a certain level of community contributions may be required.

Finally, most postgraduate applicants may demand a well-organised and detailed project proposal of the applicant's interest or donor interest. Again, pay attention to the requirements and if you have all it takes, then apply for the funds. However, do not waste your valuable time applying for the funding if you lack one of the requirements described in the advertisement because you usually not be considered. That is how strictly most funding agencies have become to enhance fairness and obtain only the eligible candidates.

Evaluation of the application is also diverse depending on the qualifications of the applicants and the demands. One of the donor agencies informed me that they usually examine each application individually regardless of the number of applicants and the first thing they look at are academic qualifications. Secondly, they evaluate the connection between their interest as a donor and the qualifications of the applicants. Likewise, they examine the project proposals (if applicable) received from the applicants and their project of interest to whether the outcomes will increase knowledge to their project or even formulate an exciting new project. Moreover, they scrutinize the applicants' current position and responsibilities in their organisations or working place, if any. They also inspect the realism of the project based on the research proposal by looking at the objectives or the research questions and the time-plan provided. Another aspect of evaluation is the usefulness and significance of the research results to the applicants, donor, community, and the applicant's organisation. Finally, they check whether the applicant fulfils all other requirements stipulated in the advertisement, such as language, gender, and geographical location (to mention a few). Therefore, the comparative and close evaluation supports them in selecting eligible and qualified candidates for the scholarships.

However, the process is endless, and that there are some requirements to observe upon receiving the scholarship. The students and the donor agency sign the contract agreeing to their partnership based on the definite requirements. It is advised for all applicants to carefully read and understand the conditions to avoid unnecessary conflict with the agencies. Some donors agencies desire to follow up with their candidates to ensure the effective use of their money and the candidate's seriousness in learning. They may apply a strategy demanding the candidate to report every semester on their academic progress to accomplish this condition. The report should come from the institution signed by a supervisor or academic administrator's concern. Different donors require different information in such a formative evaluation form, and sometimes a diverse format is applied.

So, it is vital to check the kind of information required by the donor in the formative evaluation form upon enrolment to work to meet the requirements before the reporting time.

There is also information about factors that can lead to the cancellation of the scholarship. Among the factors may be the absence of the formative evaluation report. Another prominent factor is the infringement of one of the conditions in your scholarship contract. Sometimes if you do not display the required progress, which indicates your capability of completing the study in time successfully, the situation may lead to the termination of your scholarship. You are always supposed to observe all the requirements to sustain your scholarship and build trust with your donor. Breaking off one of the conditionalities in the contract may jeopardise your right to the scholarship; it may lead to the termination of the contract and even lead to a refund of the money you have obtained so far. Therefore, it is vital to observe and follow what you have signed for your scholarship.

In some cases, the donor may ask the candidate to work for them after successful graduation (If that was among the conditions). The employment might happen based on the candidate's project outcomes and donors' interest, even if it was not part of the contract. Working for the donor after graduation is not unusual and sometimes can be a good experience for graduates' career journey. Some candidates ask for this opportunity for experience purposes and to pay back the generosity. In most cases, during the learning period, candidates create a good relationship with their donor agencies, and, for some people, the relationship may lead to feeling comfortable working together. As a scholarship recipient, you may find out with your donor whether you ought or you can work in her organisation after graduation. Looking for an employment opportunity even before graduation and within an organisation that supports and acknowledges your knowledge, skills and competencies is always beneficial. Indeed, most scholarships may end up with employment opportunities that many graduates require.

Note that: this information about the assessment procedures and the relationship between the students and the donor agencies was provided to me by three major donor agencies and may vary from other donors.

The Demand for Equity in Access to HE

Another driving force for people to join HE is the policy promoting equity in HE access (Manathunga (2009), Palmer, Davis, & Gasman (2011)). The equity policy is going hand in hand with the internationaliation of HE and massification (Guri-Rosenblit, Šebková, & Teichler (2007), Rossi (2010)). These policies have made groups under-represented in formal education and in HE favoured by the policymakers and implementers. For example, women were less represented in HE in the 1800s and early 1900s. Simpson (1983) informed us that HE was mainly for young men expected to work as engineers, lawyers, theologians, and medical doctors. It was a time for man's domination, and HE learning environment was not a pleasant place for women in most universities worldwide (Aitchison & Guerin (2014), Batliwala (1994a, 1994b), Duflo (2012)).

I heard from Susan, a female academic, who explained the situation she experienced in HE. She asserted: *"Female students were not expected to eat at the cafeteria and enjoy meals just as male students. Rather, they were anticipated to cook food for themselves and others around them in their dormitories. Therefore, female students who desired to eat at university cafeterias normally faced harassment from male students and were asked to stop violating their role as women. The harassment was related to what society perceived as women's roles, but it was a more strategic act of discrimination. It was purposive creation of an unpleasant learning environment for the females to discourage them from participating in HE. Very few female students managed to join HE, especially those who had family members working in HEIs".*

This description from Susan aligns with what happened in 1995 in one university (I do not want to mention the country, neither the university for security purposes) where a female student committed suicide due to harassment she encountered from male students. They devalued her verbally and sexually harassed her to the extent that she could not tolerate it, and she finally committed suicide. Indeed, the learning environment in most universities in the 1900s was not conducive for female students. There are many memories of the unpleasant and discriminatory treatment that female students experienced. The discriminatory acts are among the many reasons that caused many women not to join HE so, few gained a degree. However, the barrier has been minimised, and females desire to utilise the available opportunities by joining HE studies.

Therefore, the purposive measure to empower women has led to increased women's enrolment in different universities. The Beijing Conference of 1995

(United Nations, 1995), where women's problems were discussed and strategies formulated to empower women worldwide, is one of the driving forces for increasing women in HEIs. The conference proposed various measures to promote women; among the measures was to increase access to formal and higher education and encourage women to interfere with traditional "male's tables" for decision-making. Even though such women's conferences had been held before by the United Nations (1975,1985), the implementation of women's empowerment was observed mainly after the Beijing Conference of 1995 in many places worldwide (United Nations,1995).

Moreover, each country that signed the agreement had to have some strategies to ensure equality. For example, in the UK, the Equality Act of 2010 (Butler, 2016), amended in 2019, ensures all groups' rights in society, including women. Undoubtedly, HE female participation has increased, and it has changed male domination behaviour gradually. Currently, female students in most HEIs are even higher than male students in most countries and European countries (see chart 1). Besides, people have witnessed female presidents in countries that had difficulties accepting female abilities, and again, female vice president Kamala Harris, in America.

Likewise, the primary driving force for women to join HE is their desire to occupy leadership positions. After the Beijing Conference, most governments encouraged women to take some leadership positions previously for males. However, most women had no formal qualifications required for a leader because some leadership positions, in most countries, require the candidates to possess a degree. As a result, a degree has become an essential qualification apart from others the leader should possess (Bridgstock, 2009). Therefore, women who desire to be leaders, especially in public sectors, should join HE for a degree. Indeed, there is an increased interest in leadership positions among women, which might be why the increasing number of female students in HE. Likewise, there is a belief that a leader with HE might have acquired vital knowledge, skills, and competencies that are fundamental for becoming a good leader (Overtoom (2000), Tholen (2017)) than other levels of education. Therefore, this is to say that women's empowerment in different leadership positions has accelerated their enrolment to HE.

Again, increasing HE enrolment for women is facilitated by the availability of scholarships directed to women only. (See the list of scholarship agencies in appendix 1). Furthermore, as I mentioned earlier, women's empowerment in a leadership position and their participation in formal education has led some donor agencies to dedicate their effort and funds to empower women (Lopez-Claros, Zahidi & Forum économique Mondial, 2005). Indeed, most women are ambitious to join HE and occupy leadership positions, but most lack the information and funds required for education. Therefore, some donors, who desire to support women (McAdam, Harrison, & Leitch, 2018), allocate scholarships. This purposive support might also be one of the reasons for the increasing participation of females in HE learning.

Indeed, women's empowerment and access to HE needs to be prioritised without jeopardising other groups. The majority in most societies believe that children depend on their parents for proper growth, especially their mothers (Fan & Chen, 2001). They also believe that there are several disadvantages for a woman to commence HE without adequate information that can lead to better family preparation. Indeed, some students sometimes are the losers of family, friends, career, and other dearly essential things soon after enrolment. Most of the time, the loss is caused by the absence of balance between their private lives, family lives, and studies (Schultz, 1974). Consequently, after enrolment, most female students tend to focus on their studies and less on their private/family life or vice versa.

For example, I heard of a female student, Lizbeth, who had a lovely family; a husband and three children. She had an excellent relationship with her husband and children, and life was good for all of them before she commenced the HE. Her curiosity and the availability of a generous scholarship package made her decide to take a degree. Her husband was okay with the idea due to the money involved, and they decided to send their children to a boarding school while she joined a doctoral degree. Lizbeth was busy with her studies, and she could not attend all family occasions as it was before. Her husband felt lonely as most of the time; he had to attend family and other gatherings alone. He was not as busy as Lizbeth, so; he could not remain the same person; instead, he decided to find someone else to cover the gap left by his wife. It is a long story, but the whole point is that the loving family was broken up into pieces that could not be collected and form a whole thing again, and the burden was heavy for the children. Anyway, the women empowerment movement is one of the catalysts for the female to join HE.

Indeed, most women join HE with little preparation. Regardless of the family, financial, and social situation, one needs guidance from the beginning to the end of the learning journey. Remember, HE requires financial and non-financial resources such as relationships to motivate individuals to focus on their studies. HE is the most demanding and rewarding level of education to the majority, as Wisker, Robinson, Trafford, Lilly, & Warnes (2004) explained. Sometimes, a degree is attained smoothly if the individual has adequate information and is motivated to spend many hours learning almost everything, one thing, or something.

Loss of Employment

Undoubtedly, when people lose their employment, they attempt to fill their days with some activities. However, some people cannot stay home thinking and listen to what is happening in their lives. Therefore, they desire to engage in activities without thinking critically and asking vital questions about their decision. For example, in the financial crisis, epidemic, or other catastrophes, some people lose their employment or receive permission from their employers. Some obtain permissions with payment, while others do not receive payment. Some countries have a scheme that secures payment for the non-employed people; others have no such scheme of non-employment benefits. For those who have no payment during the unemployment period, it might be a desperate time for them, and that meeting with encouraging information about HE can be relieved of a kind.

However, such a period can be short or longer than expected. The person may decide to join HE with the frustration of losing a job and studying something (Course or a degree) that is not marketable. It might be that the person desires to go out of the home to avoid several issues and that it is not his custom to stay home. What I mean by "not marketable" is the course or degree which can provide a person with the knowledge and skills required in the job market for the time and in the future. Sometimes people acquire knowledge for today's consumption, and that after some time, their knowledge is no longer needed. One of the reasons is the rapid development of technology which is stealing jobs from people.

For example, Espen informed me of his failure to the job market after graduation. He joined HE for a bachelor's degree in marketing, and that he learned marketing techniques, graduated with good grades, and felt competent for marketing. However, when he started working, the change in marketing happened where people used apps for almost everything, so he had to learn how to use technology. People who did not join HE and learned to use technology for marketing perform better than him, but he is optimistic to continue learning and demonstrating his ability. He also regrets that he joined HE because he had nothing else to do, and that was a perfect way of utilizing his time. Although it is going well for him because of his willingness to learn more about his profession, not all people have the financial capacity to keep on with the change of technology. The majority get discouraged and lose hope of becoming experts in their area. Of course, if they do not learn, they become dormant and left behind. So, yes, loss of employment can force people to quickly decide to join HE and take whatever degree to fill their time.

Making Decision

It is always beneficial for anyone to decide after collecting adequate and relevant information about the HE and the institution she desires to enrol. The person also needs to understand the institution's practices from broader perspectives than the information institutions display on their web pages. Sometimes, asking people familiar with the institution and their philosophy can help acquire practical and reliable information. The process of decision-making about joining HE is worth investing time because it is like making a judgment concerning a legal case. Normally, a good judge is expected to gather adequate, relevant information about the case and comprehend the information appropriately before judgment.

Besides, the judge ought to consult all possible sources of information for more clarification and verification (where needed) before making a judgment. Often, if the judgment is made without satisfactory investigation and reliable, diverse information, the judgment might be biased and regrettable. Therefore, I believe without exaggeration that the procedures applied in legal judgment might be vital and applicable when deciding to undertake a degree today. The information one gathers before joining HE is vital for the whole learning process, and evaluating the data is a serious project. It is important because a wrong decision may lead to monetary and non-monetary loss to the individual, family, and society. Figure one reminds us of the dozen reasons that lead people to join HE today.

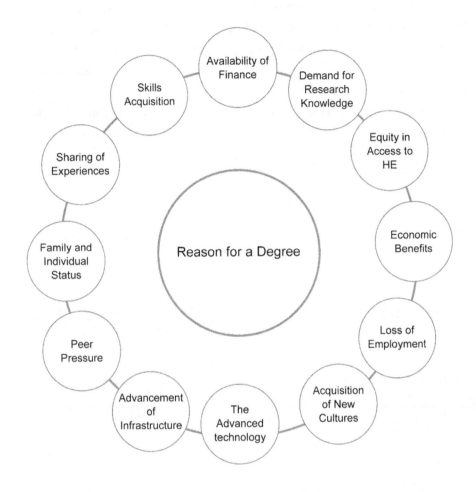

Figure 1. Dozen Reasons for People to Join HE

First, according to figure one, people decide to join HE due to technological advancement, which informs them about different opportunities. For example, people receive information about equality in learning, availability of finances for their studies, and the knowledge and skills acquired in HE. Second, others join because of better infrastructure, allowing them to choose the institution of their interest to acquire a new culture and share their experiences. Third. The majority have realized the economic benefits of a degree and the demand for research knowledge and skills. However, some have been forced to join HE due to losing employment, family status, and peer pressure.

Now, you have read about the different reasons that lead people to join HE. You have realized that some reasons are personal demands and others are from outside. However, the emphasis is that no matter where the motivation emanates from, external or internal, the investigation should be conducted for smooth learning and safely attaining the intended learning goals. Therefore, if you intend to join HE or your loved ones, it is time for you to reflect on the reasons before commencing.

You can examine your situation by responding to the following dozen questions.

Self-Reflection

Do you need a degree?

Where do you desire to learn? (Abroad or in your country), and why

What kind of responsibilities do you have in your personal/family/social?

What kind of employment responsibilities do you have?

What skills, knowledge, and competencies do you desire to acquire?

How are you going to finance your studies?

Where do you plan to apply your skills, competencies, and knowledge after graduation?

What changes do you anticipate personally and socially to meet HE demands?

What are the consequences that might happen in your life due to the study you desire to pursue?

How will you tackle the problems that may arise in your personal/family life, while you are studying?

Do you have the support you need from your peer, family, and friends?

What effort, time, and resources are you ready to utilise in your studies?

Go ahead if you have thought about the mentioned questions, have satisfactory answers, and are convinced that you need a degree. You need to think about where (abroad or in your country) and how (physical or online learning)? It is also a good decision if you decide not to join, HE if you lack preparation. You can opt to read the rest of the book for more information about HE to support you when you are ready. Even if you are not planning for, HE, the knowledge in this book may support you in advising other people around you.

Chapter III
The Main Changes in Higher Education

Structures and Practices

In more than two decades, people have witnessed changes in structure and practices in most HEIs. The rapid increase of students and their diversity have brought many changes and challenges in HE (Lee & Danby (2012), Maassen, Nokkala, & Uppstrm (2004), Marek & Peter (2012)). Likewise, the increased number of HE stakeholders (Park, 2007) who directly or indirectly influence students learning and finances have also changed the practices of HEIs. People who desire to join HE, including the students, need to be conscious of the changes in HE for better preparation and adjustment.

My desire is for people to be aware of the current HE practices. The knowledge is vital because if the existing changes are not discussed and known by stakeholders in advance, it may take them by surprise and become a stumbling block for those who desire a degree. Kharouf and Daoud (2019) asserted that most HE students spend their first year comprehending their academic context and how the institution and learning agency function. Scholars' statement means the students lack information about HE practices before enrolment and need time to comprehend different issues and adjust to the learning environment before focusing on their studies. I believe the reading of this book and the application of advice within may shorten the time proposed by these scholars. Therefore, I will discuss the significant changes in the structures and practices of HE to support the readers with vital information.

Diverse Structures and Practices

I have to acknowledge that the practices of HE have become diverse with many opportunities and challenges. There is no uniformity in implementing learning that fits for all degree programs, neither institutions nor nations. Sawir (2011) has discussed the effect of diverse practices and perceptions about international students. The scholar demonstrated the changes in structure and practices in most HEIs that can be worthy of reading for learning. Undeniably, some departments, institutions, and even countries are practicing HE learning differently based on the nature of students, the required knowledge locally and globally. The variation in demand is the main reason for having several diversities in the practices and the provision of degrees. Regardless of the European Union motive and effort of standardising HE through the Bologna agreement (EURASHE (European Ministers in charge of Higher Education) (2016), Helguero-Balcells (2009), Keeling (2006)), still, universities operate differently. Therefore, the diverse stakeholders' perceptions and demands have resulted in diverse structures and practices.

Consequently, there are significant changes (Lee & Dunston (2011), Usher (2002)) and differences from one university to the other and from a country to others. Countries, institutions, departments, and disciplines mainly fulfil their local needs, although they are sensitive to international and global qualification requirements. (Blumenthal (1996), Carter (2014), Czinkota & Ronkainen (2011), Usher & Savino (2006)). Indeed, the diverse structure and practices produce different learning outcomes and graduates quantitatively and qualitatively. To understand the changes, we must categorise HE into two categories: while comparing their practices, the traditional era (the 1900s) and the modern era (the 2000s). These practices are different, although there is no clear separation of the two. The slight or significant changes in some HEIs are the main factor that supports us in looking at these two eras as the separate timeline for HE. I will not discuss the structure of HE in terms of years required for a degree, leadership, and administration issues in this book, but I will only focus on learning practices.

Traditional Era of Higher Education

We learn from the history of HE, as discussed by Simpson (1983) in his book *"How the Ph.D. Came to Britain,"* that higher education was established to produce skilled laborers who could solve societal problems scientifically. He pointed out that Germany was the first country to introduce HE and the Ph.D., followed by the United States of America and Britain. This idea of HE establishment and professional labour production is supported by different scholars such as Kelly (2010), Clark (2007), Craswell (2007), Dalziel (2017).

These scholars discussed the purpose of HE align with the foundation of HE and have a common thought that HEIs still develop, nurture, and produce knowledgeable and skilled labour for societal development.

Hence, the major goal of most HEIs was to provide service to society through the knowledge acquired by the graduates. For example, according to one university lecturer, in the United States, HEIs were known for providing services where graduates engaged in societal issues, such as religion, politics, and education, and they created peer stewardship of leaders who could solve complex problems. The provision of service to society by the graduates was the primary motive for establishing HE in the USA. In Germany, academics were active in politics and industrial activities (Simpson (2010)) where they shared their knowledge while criticising non-scientific decisions and implementations. The voice from these founder countries acknowledged that HE is vital as a factory for producing skilled labourers.

Simpson (2010), referring to the work of John Brubacher and Willis Rudy in *A* history *of American* colleges *and Universities 1636-1976* where they provided information about HE evolution in America. Simpson contended that after the American Civil War, society demanded a shift in the role of HEIs and their contributions. Hence, it required more innovative and scientific knowledge to solve the problems people encountered at that time. Therefore, more and more universities, including the University of Chicago and Clark University, implemented making research subject one of the main focuses for students' learning. According to Simpson (ibid), this inspiration was brought to America by the American graduates who studied in Germany. This change of HE practices by focusing more on research training changed the role of HEIs not only in Germany and America but worldwide. There are different perspectives about this practice, and I will start by directing the discussion in ten significant aspects which one should bear in mind when attempting to comprehend the traditional era of HE.

Institutions and Academics Autonomy

Historically HE academics had self-autonomy over students' learning, according to Professor Samuel, my informant. The faculties could decide the courses to be studied and the number of students to supervise. The students' supervision was constructed differently, and the supervisors had the autonomy to decide when students were ready for graduation based on their progress and assessment. The supervisors were keen on whether the students had acquired the required skills required and to the level and standard expected. Teachers' autonomy was supported by David, who was also one of my informants, where he discussed his experiences with his supervisor when he was undertaking a degree in medicine. His supervisor was almost everything and everyone to him; the supervisor could ask David to work with assignments in the laboratory, even on weekends. In addition, the supervisor was responsible for evaluating each activity and proposed to David the workshops and seminars he thought were beneficial for him, even though such events were limited those days. Therefore, such a supervisor's power was vivid for almost all institutions in different departments and disciplines, especially at the doctoral level. The supervisor could assess and recommend the extended learning time for their students with little or even no interference from the institution management. This informant's explanation aligns with what scholars Manathunga (2005), Connell & Manathunga (2012) discussed as the privacy practices in supervision of research students.

In the case of doctoral degrees, a supervisor, in most universities, could be the sole source of students' academic support. In many universities, there was no advanced technology for generic online programmes (Carter, 2014) where students could communicate with other learning agencies, and that is why supervisors were essential and resourceful learning agents. Moreover, most institutions' management respected the supervisor's decision about the time required for formative and summative students' evaluations, and the supervisors had the last decision in such student's assessment. David, the one I mentioned earlier, could not remember the institute administrators or managers questioning his supervisor's decisions a single time. Indeed, professors had to observe ethics and work with high integrity regardless of the autonomy they had. Unfortunately, some academics violated the trust institutions' management had for them and no inspection or monitoring of their practices. That is why Connell and Manathunga (2012) inform poor supervision was the weakness of the old universities' practices.

As I pointed out earlier, there is no clear cut between the traditional era and the modern era of HE. Scholars have recently informed us that supervision in the modern era is also a personal pedagogy or personal business between a supervisor and a student (Manathunga, 2005). The supervision pedagogy also created challenges associated with relationships between the partners that may collide with historical background and experiences between the students and the supervisors (Grant (2003, 2005, 2008). However, the supervision relationship has been hierarchical since the formation of HE and most universities management seem satisfied with supervisors' practices. Contrary, we read from the literature that supervisors often do not fulfill their responsibilities (Connell & Manathunga, 2012), Lee (2007), Grant 2008)). Supervision and supervisors' autonomy over students were observed in the traditional era and still demonstrated in the modern era of HE.

In addition, institutions had autonomy over the employment of their academics and how to finance them. My informant, the experienced Professor Lee, argued that almost every HE institution in this country and many countries had a way of practicing students learning without government interference. He asserted: *"HEIs had the authority to plan what they desired to teach to their students, how to teach, and who should teach. All the procedures from students' enrolment to the graduations were formulated, implemented, and monitored by the institutions using their academics. The employment contracts were also different and more secure than today, where we work with a contract. Besides, the institutions formulated policies focusing on enhancing students' learning, the local community, and the nation's interests. The institutions and academics were aware of society's skills, knowledge, and competencies and adjusted learning accordingly. Today universities have no autonomy, but most governments desire to control the practice of HEIs and plan their operations, including student learning contents and time for learning. Likewise, most HEIs are full of foreign academics who have little knowledge of community needs and sometimes lack students' interest."*

This explanation indicates the changes in autonomy from academics and institutions to government control. It also indicates the existence of foreign learning and teaching arena for HE practitioners that one should bear in mind.

It was Gender Bias

Traditionally, HE was gender-biased, and only young men were expected to attain a degree in most universities. These young men were trained to be the stewards of their discipline (Simpson, 1983), and females were not part of HE territory. I pointed out about gender issue and the changes that have been happening since the Beijing conferences briefly in the previous chapter, such as female scholarships and leadership position opportunities. Therefore, gender discrimination was societal and culturally structured due to, among others, the separate role females and males had in most communities. Indeed, gender responsibilities differentiated males and females, where men were expected to make vital decisions in family/private lives and public (Lindsey, 2015). For instance, the leadership positions, teaching, advocate, and medical professions were among the male jobs, and these were the disciplines where the first degrees were established. These professionals usually have high responsibilities, status, and privileges economically and socially compared to other service provision positions.

The dominance of males of specific classes in HE was vivid; for example, in Canada, Jones (2014) quoted the work of Neatby and asserted:

"Universities trained the children of the political elites; they served as a finishing school for their daughters and prepared their sons for admission to the liberal professions. Governments and university officials understood these social functions; there were no major confrontations over admissions, course content, or student discipline because both groups shared the same social values. Cabinet ministers and members of the Board of Governors might belong to different parties, but they were all men of substance with similar views of the social order"(p. 34)

The statement indicates another common feature these young men had and the families they came from. The major qualification was the cultural background, status in the community, including the family. This information was unclear to me, and I asked one informant, Jovel, about this statement, and he argued: *"Of course, people with low income and lacked exposure, at that time, were struggling with life, and they had no information of what was going on at universities neither interested in education. Besides, the majority were not financially capable of enrolling their children in HE and had no education themselves. Therefore, university education was for a few who were aware of the benefits associated with HE and had money to pay for the education. Most of these people had high social positions, such as university teachers, religious leaders, medical doctors, and politicians. We can generally say that most of the students came from elite families."*

Undeniably, several kinds of literature indicate that HE was for a few privileged males (Clark (2007), Kelly (2017), Simpson (1983)). Society expected that these male graduates could teach, research, and ensure justice in the communities. The females had less influence and sometimes no influence at all in most decisions. For example, I read one book; I do not remember the title, the author described the transport situation in the 1980s in most cities in Europe. He explained that all buses and trains were full of men from 04:00 to 09:00 am going to work while women (where necessary) could be seen publicly after nine going to the market to buy some cooking stuff for the families. If this was the situation in Europe, one could easily generalise that women's situation in many countries worldwide. However, in Africa, in many countries, women were the ones to wake up early and deal with the family operation. So, the division of labour was unquestionable and one aspect that facilitated the domination of male students in most universities while females were left behind. Certainly, HE learning was mainly for males to perform leadership roles and solve other societal problems. At that time, knowledge concerning women's capability in problem-solving was shallow, and people did not believe in women. In contrast, females were believed capable of caring for families and that except them from other crucial decision-making tables, including participating in HE.

Less Government Involvement

The same professor discussed institutions' autonomy; Lee contended: *"Most governments were not much involved in making academic decisions. Educational institutions were preserved for professionals, and they had their rituals to observe without interference from external agencies. In most cases, the institution leadership, board members and academics were autonomous in their decisions."*

Indeed, according to my informants, most HEIs functioned with confidence without many governmental interferences and conditionalities from donor agencies. He added:

"For example, most institutions employed academics they thought could meet students' learning needs and that they stipulated employment rules and regulations that suited their learning environments. The institutions had autonomy over the use of resources required in learning, and the evaluation of students' formative and summative was conducted based on the institution's standards and preferences. They also certified students based on their values and standards that they considered important to ensure students' knowledge, skills, and competencies. These rituals were vital in HEIs and for students even though they were not financially beneficial. Besides, students learning was not much directed to international interests even though some countries cooperated."

Institutional autonomy is among the practices that most HEIs have lost; the independence of institutions and faculties has almost gone. Instead, in most countries and universities, the governments' hand is so heavy that sometimes it becomes unbearable.

Service-Oriented University

Although teachers in HE had freedom and autonomy, their contributions to knowledge were based on service. The role of supervisors was in line with the role of HEIs to provide service to society with less focus on the personal and institutional economic profits. According to Connell and Manathunga (2012), some university teachers were assigned supervision responsibilities without being rewarded, and that supervision was not considered part of the teaching workload. Besides, teachers were not training how to supervise to support them to become good supervisors (Wisker, 2005, 2012); instead, supervision was something to learn by observation. Supervisors were expected to supervise students as they were self-supervised (Connell & Manathunga (2012), Grant (2005), Lee (2007)). As a result, some avoid bad experiences and focus on being the best supervisors to their students by providing the service they did not obtain. Others could not differentiate unpleasant experiences and hence transferred whatever they observed in their supervision to their students.

Indeed, there are different stories about the old universities' practices. For instance, I heard of this professor, who explained his experiences as a university teacher in the old days. He asserted that university teachers in Europe and even America received little payments than other professionals who had a degree, such as lawyers and medical doctors. He described the hardship of life for most university teachers where some were supposed to work for many hours with little payments. He even informed that most of these brilliant teachers had to teach, sometimes, more than one institution and in their private time to pay their bills. Moreover, some teachers had no holidays as they used for those who needed extra tuition, and mainly because teaching job was regarded as a service. The motives of many teachers were to observe their students succeed, and knowledge was to be shared almost for free. Therefore, academics were expected to contribute to society with knowledge as a service, not as a commercial good.

In addition, people desired to earn a degree to acquire the skills required in solving societal problems. Similarly, graduates were expected to support their communities with their knowledge because people who acquired a degree tend to occupy vital positions in society, and because of that, they managed to apply their knowledge as expected. Thus, the concept of service aligns with what Bourdieu (1990) and Neveu (2018) described education as capital and its importance in human development. They asserted that education and HE are among the capital that may benefit individuals to gain other capitals such as culture, social, and even symbolic capital. Indeed, HE increases the ability of graduates to contribute to individuals and society in problem-solving, which accelerates development. Likewise, the history described by Simpson (1983) demonstrates that HE graduates had a legitimate power to criticise unscientific knowledge and implementations for better service to their societies.

Specialisation Learning

Traditionally, students were supposed to focus on a specific discipline. The primary aim for specialisation was to ensure that students become experts in a specific area and the stewards of the field. The most recognised fields of study for a degree were theology, mathematics, medicine, and law (Simpson, 1983). The individuals were expected to focus on one discipline with little or no interdisciplinary connections (Clark (2007) Manathunga, Lant, & Mellick, (2006). For example, teachers in most HEIs specialised in a single discipline with little or no interaction with members of other departments (Clark (2007), Simpson (1983)). Refer to the mentioned disciplines where an individual could have acquired a degree, and that is how they were expected to be a field steward. Connell & Manathunga (2012) admitted that there was no interaction with another discipline or learning agencies from different departments. The separation of disciplines was both for students and the faculties; people were focusing on their discipline. Connell postulate:

"It was largely me kicking on and doing it, without any interaction with the other students in the department about our theses (p. 5)."

Therefore, teachers in the department were the only facilitators the students could consult in case of support. The sources of knowledge were limited to students, and most of the time, students were recipients of the knowledge from their supervisors and the transmitter of the knowledge to the future generation (Grant (2005), Manathunga (2005)). Likewise, some students, especially research students, had no access and freedom to contact other learning agencies after being assigned a supervisor. The learning becomes a private matter between the partners (Manathunga, 2005), and as a result, students specialised in specific disciplines, contents, and thoughts.

The "Goddesses" of Supervisors

Concerning teachers' autonomy, most supervisors portrayed themselves as goddesses to students (Manathunga, 2005). There were several barriers students had to cross in their learning posed by their goddesses. If they desired to succeed, the essential students had to work closely with their supervisors (refer to David's experience). Most research students worked in the shadow of their supervisor, and the challenges they faced in supervision received less attention (Grant & Mckinley (2011), Grant (2008)). Since some students had only one supervisor who had all power over them and was the determinant of students' progress, achievement, and qualifications, their position became like that of gods. The supervisor was the person to allow or hinder students' graduation based on his assessment, hence giving academic life. However, Connell & Manathunga (2012) describes this kind of supervision as unsuccessful because it sometimes leads to the abandonment of students where the supervisor and the institutions made little effort to support students' learning. At the same time, students were expected to acquire the required qualifications miraculously. Commenting about Ph.D. supervision, the scholars asserted:

"They (institutional officials) didn't count Ph.D. supervision as any part of an academic workload either. It was as if you did this by a kind of divine aura around you as a scholar, and the student would stand close and get warmed by this (p. 5)."

The fact is the supervision task was not considered a task that required serious attention from a supervisor. At the same time, students' graduation depended on the supervisors' satisfaction with students' formative and summative learning outcomes.

Flexible Completion Time

The supervisor was the one to determine the completion time for research students. There was no time pressure for students' completion as it is today where at most master's degree is allocated two years and doctorate three years in humanities degrees. The teachers were the ones who could legitimise the students' learning progress and the quality of students' knowledge without jeopardising their performance or employment. The evaluation practice was

71

based on the social role universities played at that time. The informant, whom I mentioned earlier, David, undertook Ph.D. studies in medicine for more than seven years, and he received no pressure to complete his project. He worked with his supervisor ensuring the mastering of the required learning materials and the acquisition of knowledge and skills required of him and those he desired to acquire. The supervisor was all around him, criticizing his perceptions and supporting him correctly to achieve the degree. In the old days, according to Connell and Manathunga (2012), students managed to rethink and rewrite their work creatively due to, among others, the flexibility that existed in the completion time. Finally, David's supervisor was the one who recommended him for employment as a teacher in medical at the same university he studied at.

Uni-Culture Learning Environment

As mentioned earlier, HE's learning environment was western culture. The learning environment was based on a single culture where most students had a similar background, European background, from Germany, Britain, and the USA. Afterward, there were minority students from other European countries, but according to Simpson (1983), no student recorded coming from other continents such as Africa and Asia studying in Germany in those early days of HE. The culture difference mentioned in the old days was that of Americans (Afro-American) at the University of Yale, Pennsylvania, Harvard, and Princeton (Simpson, 1983). The continents Africa and Asia established HE alongside the spread of European culture through colonialism.

Most institutions in Africa and Asia experienced the educational culture of the colonies. When I studied for a master's degree in Comparative and International Education, I also realised that the education system of most countries in Africa and Asia follows either the American, French, or British system. Therefore, students in the early days studied mainly in their continent and within the limited learning culture. The idea of uni-culture aligns with what Manathunga and Connell (2012) indicated when discussing learning at the doctoral level. They described different aspects that indicate that the traditional HE learning was based on the European culture's single cultural environment.

The uni-culture had been the practice of many institutions until globalisation[3] [1]was implemented (Gary, Robert & Ray (2001), Hensley, Galilee-Belfer, & Lee (2013)). This policy was implemented in HE through internationalisation; thus, it integrates international or intercultural perspectives into HE learning, teaching, and research (Van Der Wende, 2007). The process allows the exchange of knowledge and cultures through the collaboration of students and academics across countries and continental borders. This intellectual cooperation in knowledge has become the catalyst for accommodating diverse cultures in most HEIs and hence the change from uni-culture to multiculturalism.

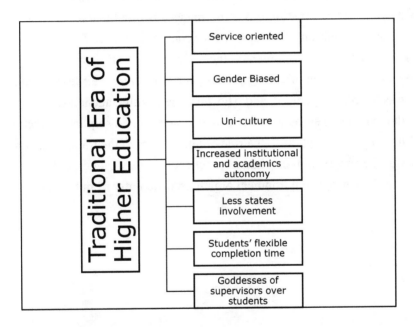

Figure 2. The Nature of the Traditional Era of Higher Education

According to figure two, the old era of HE had the following features; first, there was a gender bias where only young men with elite backgrounds had access to education. Second, the institutions operate under uni-culture, European culture, and education focused on service with flexible students' completion time,

---

[3]As a concept in education refers to the condensation of the world intellectually across borders with the notion of sharing knowledge and skills through learning, teaching, and researching.

institutions and faculties autonomy, and less governments' involvement. These aspects are few of many that differentiate the old days' universities and the modern.

Self-Reflection

Do you have any family members who acquired a degree in the early 1900s?
What were the experiences you have heard for the students and faculties concerning the traditional HE era?
Are you aware of the practices of most HEIs concerning enrolment?
How do you think the institutions were financed before the internationalisation?
What was the condition of women in your country about HE?
What was the role of government in the early 1900s in HE learning?
What was the situation of teachers in HE, and what were their leading roles?
How was learning organised, and who were the learning agencies?
How did the relationship between the departments and discipline's function?
How do people conceptualise the role of universities in the traditional era?
How was the supervision of students practiced and its weaknesses?
How was the learning environment organised differently from today?

Chapter IV
Modern Era of Higher Education

The previous chapter has reminded us of seven major issues that dominated HE in the old days. However, some changes have occurred in HE practices contrary to the history described. One thing for sure is that it might be difficult to mention all the changes that have occurred. However, I will mention eleven significant changes that I consider vital to share and that are vital for readers to comprehend before commencing in HE. It is beneficial to understand these changes even if you have already enrolled because the information may support you understand some of the practices in advance. For example, knowing how HE learning practice was organised in the traditional era and the changes will prepare you to find gaps to fill. I have to repeat that the major aim of the discussion in this book is to convey the information to facilitate readers for a simple decision-making process and success in learning for those who desire to acquire a degree. Indeed, the modern era of HE has been different from the traditional era and is still in motion.

Besides, the changes in HE in this book are not universal. They vary from one institution to another, a country to others, and even from a continent to others. Some may extend traditional practices, and hence there is no clear cut of these practices, but there are indeed changes. The alteration may also be experienced differently, based on the context, the nature of learning agencies, government involvement, and the institutions' learning culture. However, the book focuses on common changes that affect students learning worldwide and affect HE stakeholders.

However, if you are clear about which institution you want to enroll, then you have to find more and specific information about the institution's current learning practices. The changes are not discussed based on their importance or effect on students learning, but I write them in response to the historical era with no other intentions.

Higher Education is for All

The discourses of equity in education have permeated in HE. As I mentioned earlier, HE was for young men and not for women (Simpson, 1983). Current, HEIs' doors are open to everybody regardless of gender and other demographic factors that hindered many before. Today people of all gender, ages, and economic statuses have access to HE upon meeting the criterion required, including academic results and finances associated with learning. The increased HE access is among the many changes in HE influenced by the internationalisation of HE through economic, social, and political cooperation's, as described by Braathe & Otterstad (2014).

Therefore, many countries aim at increasing the number of their graduates by supporting them with funds. For instance, some governments have used welfare schemes as financial tools to support people to acquire a degree (Kivinen & Ahola, 1999). The scholars, Kivinen, Hedman & Kaipainen (2007) have also demonstrated the strategies to expand education access from elite to all. Furthermore, in most countries, especially in the west and north, the governments also accommodate local and international students with diverse backgrounds and support them financially. The universities provide different grants and scholarships for many students who lack finance for their education using different criteria. Although some international students have different learning needs, expectations, and experiences than local ones, they should cooperate in learning. In some universities, these students receive support to cope with the local learning environment and enhance knowledge society, as Valimaa & Hoffman (2008) explained.

Access to HE has increased students' movements locally and globally. Several academics have demonstrated the increasing enrolment of people from all backgrounds. Students from developing countries or even countries with advanced economies can enroll in the institution of their choice worldwide (although it is still an erratic movement). For example, the European countries, the US, and other countries are strengthening HE internationalisation, leading to increased access to education for all. Some scholars (Doyle, Manathunga, Prinsen, Tallon & Cornforth (2017), Maassen et al. (2004), Maringe & Foskett (2012), Van der Wende (2007)). Although some scholars have documented the effect of internationalisation on the quality of education, this has not hindered the increased number and diversity of students and academics in the HE learning environment.

Students' mobility to North America and Europe has led to the rapidly increasing number of students in these continents. For instance, in 2016, the European HE statistic (Eurostat) indicated the increasing number of students, as shown in Chart 1.

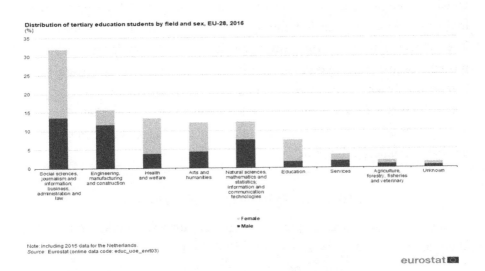

Distribution of tertiary education students by field and sex, EU-28, 2016
(%)

Note: including 2015 data for the Netherlands.
Source: Eurostat (online data code: educ_uoe_enrt03)

eurostat

The chart shows an increasing number of female and male students in HE in 2016. Most students preferred to study social science, journalism, and information, while others favoured engineering and natural science. It also indicates that more male students were in natural science fields than females while female students dominated education, arts, and humanities. The field of agriculture, forestry, fisheries, veterinary, and services had fewer students compared to other fields. These are among the fields that traditionally, their practitioners did not need a degree. However, because research is needed in all areas of humans activities, the universities had to establish degrees in these fields. In addition, the statistics indicated that generally, the number of female students in European HEIs had increased rapidly compared to the male students. Most students originate from Africa, America, Asia, Europe, and Oceania. So, the trend diverges from the traditional HE where only a few students of the same ethnicity (Simpson, 1983) were enrolled in HE to diverging population.

Indeed, some scholars support the increasing number and diversity of students and academics positively. For instance, Walker & Thomson Ed. (2010) regarded diversity as a learning opportunity to generate imaginative knowledge and skills required locally and globally. Likewise, Manathunga (2017) regarded internationalisation as a huge opportunity when she asserted that "the time has come where knowledge from the South, East, and indigenous should have its contribution through purposive scholars' and students' interactions." The diverse collaborations have made the learning environment in HE to be a zone of multicultural meetings, mainly through research activities (Manathunga, 2009). The scholar indicated that the environment where all knowledge is welcomed provides an excellent opportunity for students, participants, and academics to benefit from each other. These experiences might create more unity and global cooperation in education and social and economic sectors. The idea of students' and academics' movement and access to foreign HEIs are among the strategies that have enhanced HE for all.

Multidiscipline Degree Design

Moreover, the degree practices diverge toward multidiscipline from undisciplined. Most universities allow students to take whatever course they desire apart from the compulsory courses of their discipline. The accessibility to diverse courses is possible because the learning agencies and programmes are diverse, and teaching is no longer solely the teachers' responsibility (Carter (2014), Crebert et al. (2004). For example, in most universities, as informed by a course coordinator, Jane, from a university, they have different programmes online that support students' learning. The programmes are sometimes individually, and group structured where students can attend workshops and seminars on their pace and convenience if they need clarification of the contents online. Jane asserted: *"A student of humanity or language can be interested in learning a course provided in the science department or vice versa. The student can enrol in the course he desired without the consent of a supervisor. Besides, students have access to courses and programmes provided by the university online regardless of the field of study."*

These systems i.e.; online programmes, seminars, and workshops, have created a vast opportunity for students to learn courses from other faculties and fields (multi-discipline) and have broadened their interaction and thoughts when interacting with various learning agencies. The multidisciplinary environment supports students in acquiring diverse knowledge that can be applied in diverse fields for problem-solving. Besides, having diverse knowledge from different fields is an advantage for HE graduates' employability. Indeed, this is a change opposing the traditional form of learning designed for a single discipline and limited to a single learning agency, faculty.

Knowledge as a Commodity

The trade of intellectuals between and among countries is the real issue. Scholars term this knowledge imperialism (Collins (2007), Kostrykina, Lee, & Hope (2017)), where western countries are interchanging scholarship for intellectuals with less developed countries (refer to appendix 1 for scholarship), sometimes, developing countries gain nothing. Indeed, the accumulation of intellectuals to the west and north results from an even movement of students. The problem is also discussed by Van Der Wende (2015), Wu & Zha (2018) where they both indicated the business associated with intellectual movement and how this movement has affected the service notion of HE. Higher education stakeholders should also comprehend that the movement of academics has not been observed in such a fashion before the internationalisation of HE. The trend may be a threat because HE graduates are the source of the skilled workforce of any society. Most intellectuals from developing countries tend to remain in developed countries after graduation and hence brain drain.

The HE business affects students directly due to their position as primary consumers. Most students must borrow money from banks or other sources to finance their education. In addition, the tuition fees are high in most HEIs (you can search information in different universities' web pages about the fees for a degree), and international students pay for expenses associated with accommodation, transports, and other services required in a foreign country. For example, in Canada, according to Brownlee (2005) in his article *"Corporatisation and Commercialisation, Public Policy,"* asserted:

"While tuition varies considerably across provinces, the overall cost of undergraduate tuition has grown from an average of $1,706 in 1991-92 to $6,191 in 2015-16, an increase of 263 percent. Escalating fees) has also meant escalating student debt" (p. 3).

Indeed, it is expensive to acquire a degree, and that is why one should have adequate information of the structure, practices of the institution, and the benefits the degree brings to the individual and society. Brownlee (2005) added that:

"Federal government student loan debt in Canada is approximately $15 billion. When provincial and commercial bank loans are included, the total is closer to $20 billion." (p. 3).

This information indicates how costly HE has become and that the burden is on the shoulder of the consumer, students (their families, of course) who are the buyers of education. Certainly, the increase of students and the movement of students from less wealthy countries to the wealthy and the expenses associated with education is evidence that there is an evenly business between the rich and the poor, as Kortrykina and Svetlana (2017) explained. However, benefiting from the poor seems enjoyable to rich countries and may raise ethical questions that may lead to mistrust.

However, without a doubt, education commercial is a worldwide business. Even isolated countries of the world, through advanced technology and other advanced infrastructures, are reachable in this business and accommodate many students from other parts of the world. For example, New Zealand, one of the isolated countries in the global, has increased the number of international doctoral students from 47325 in 2005 to 61430 in 2015 (MoETE, 2017). I picked New Zealand because it was inaccessible and had no tradition of enrolling students from all parts of the world. Most of my informants inform the popularity of continents like Europe and America, and some are familiar with Australia as learning destinations. Therefore, one may see changes, and that most governments and even peripheral aim to increase international students to boost their economy. The governmental objectives and the process, including their strategies of increasing the knowledge economy, are no longer an underground issue (Greenberg (2018), Nada & Araújo (2018)).

So, to ensure benefits, the cost of education for international students is high. However, it varies from one country to another and the institution to others depending on the discipline. Likewise, the practice of paying for education and the trade between the rich and the developing countries has eroded the notion of service provision while creating a business arena. Most students from developing countries have to pay for education when studying in rich countries by themselves or through grants and scholarships. Therefore, countries with sophisticated infrastructure, including technology, attract individuals from other countries with the opposite circumstances, hence business.

The Role of Higher Education Institutions

According to economic benefits, the role of HE has changed from a service organisation to an organisation for development. As I mentioned earlier, HE in the traditional era was expected to serve society with knowledge. Indeed, less focus was directed to economic gain through the knowledge provided, and HEIs were not regarded as agencies for nations' economics promoters. However, current HEIs are industries known for nations' sources of the economy through what scholars term as a knowledge economy (Connell (2015), Gokhberg, Meissner, & Shmatko (2017), Kostrykina et al. (2017), Pedersen (2014)). For example, as mentioned earlier, most western universities are accessed by tuition payment, and that students have to pay for every service (accommodation, transport, upkeep) they obtain during their learning. Therefore, even though some students from non-western countries receive scholarships, the majority have to borrow money from banks or any other sources to access HE.

I had a conversation with two administrators in one university, Donald, who asserted that: "*International students are major assets of our country and other countries that host them.*" Asking what they benefit from students, one contended: "*Students have to pay for their transport, accommodation, social events, foods, clothing, books, medical care, and other services they need. All these sectors employ people who provide services, and that bring income to our country.*" Another Christopher pointed out specifically the issue of accommodation: "*It is difficult to get accommodation near universities these days, and if you get, it tends to be of a higher price than other areas. For instance, people with houses around the university are benefitting from their housing in our country.*

On top of that, some students tend to work part-time, they pay taxes, even though the payment they receive is lower than other people. Besides, students are effective with time and more productive than other groups, and their payment is not as high as other workers; they allow themselves to be cheap labourers. Apart from that, all the publications and knowledge produced by students during their studies belong to the University. Therefore, although we observe intellectuals' rights, this varies from one department to another, the level of students' participation plays a part of their own, and the nature of knowledge produced or discovery."

This explanation aligned with what scholars have acknowledged the benefits western governments obtain through tertiary education, trade (Kostrykina et al., 2017; Van Der Wende, 2015). The main strategy for many western countries is to increase the number of international students. Therefore, HEIs are no longer service provider organizations, but they are the source of national economic development. Knowledge is exchanged with money and other services through the knowledge economy concept (Valimaa & Hoffman, 2008). Indeed, several changes have occurred in HE to facilitate and justify the phenomenon of the knowledge economy. The change in the roles of universities has also altered the provision of educational services focusing on the economic benefits.

Stakeholders' demands

Another change in HE is the stakeholders and their demands. In the previous discussion, I discussed scholarships and donor agencies' preferences. It has turned out that most governments are also among the leading and reliable donors for HE financing in some countries, the governments remain the only reliable and consistent donor (Kivinen & Ahola, 1999). Having this vital position, most governments have become donors and the major stakeholders who make legitimate decisions, stipulate policies, and other requirements that institutions must observe. Currently, most decisions in many HEIs, where the government is the prominent donor, are made by the governments, and that institutions, through academics, and students has to implement the decisions and conditions to obtain the funds.

For example, according to Jones (2014), in Canada, HE is the most centralised system of education, and the government engages in research, training, and retraining of the workforce and funding education for ages. It is said that this increase of the governmental immersion in HEIs is significant and is caused by, among others, the increase in foreign employees. One lecturer, Lee, through a telephone conversation with me, contended that:

"We foreigners, we are experts in this country, and we do our job of teaching and supervising students in their projects, but we tend to avoid engaging ourselves in the politics beyond the university philosophy. The separation from other issues in the community may be advantageous for most of us but a disadvantage for our students because learning is not only in the curriculum or learning programs but also in society and its concerns. Understanding the

challenges people encounter outside universities and the debates in society might be the added advantage of academics in their guidance role. Therefore, knowing society's concerns may create the best opportunity for the research topic and solve several problems in society. I believe teachers who understand society and its politics outside the university, and the real-life of people and the students, can lead students better than those with limited information and involvement in society. My explanation is not to undermine the expertise many of us possess, but I understand the importance of government involvement in our institution and others."

The information by Lee can respond to the question; why most government involvement has increased in many universities today? I would think the governments needed to make sure that the education community and the rest of the society are inseparable and that there is an integration between the knowledge acquired and needed by the community. Indeed, governments' involvement is observed in many countries these days than ever before because of, among others, what Lee described as monitoring HEIs practices. For example, in Australia, Kiley (2011) discussed three dimensions that the government focuses on: first is to reduce attrition of students in HE, second is, to reduce their learning time by emphasising timely completion, and third is to increase their satisfaction and their experiences in learning (this was for postgraduate students). The direction, policies, and orders are the kind of leadership the government has provided to institutions for implementation.

In Nordic countries, Maassen, Nokkala & Uppstrm (2004) described governments' involvement in HE as more than ever before. However, scholars have also demonstrated that sometimes governments' viewpoints tend to conflict with the actual experiences academics and students encounter. For example, there is a discussion on whether the funding policies associated with students' timely degree completion formulated by states jeopardise students' learning and the quality of human resources produced by the universities. Consequently, there is a concern about the absence of academics and institutions' autonomy even though they are the ones who implement the policies stipulated by the government. As the main actors, academics and students might understand the situation in HE better than the government officials then how to cooperate may be a challenge.

There are some different arguments concerning government involvement in HE learning worldwide. For example, some academics believe that governments are making policies that focus more on the economic benefit (Lee (2007), Stensaker et al. (2008) than ensuring students' learning. It has been observed further that although students and academics are the significant implementers of institutional and governmental policies, they are less involved in formulating HE learning policies (Kiley (2011), OECD (2018), Stensaker et al. (2008).

Certainly, students' and academics' voices are less heard even on the issues related to the psychosocial learning environments where they are the leading performers. For example, Lee (2007) describes the current HE learning environment as super complex where the needs of academics and students are less considered. The scholar discussed the pressure in the relationship among HE stakeholders, including students and supervisors, that is believed to be accelerated by governmental funding policies (timely students' completion). In general, the scholar emphasised the quality of supervisors and the graduates. Therefore, governmental and institutional policy formulation should focus on students learning benefits.

Increase Number of Students in HEIs

Increasingly, many people join HE, and most universities observe the effect of "massification" (refer to chart nr.1). For universities to fulfil HE for all policy, they have allowed all groups of people who meet the requirements to join HE, and that universities accommodate a considerable number of students. Most scholars discuss the effect this increasing number of students has caused on the quality of supervision and education in general. For instance, Lee (2007) asserts:

"The range of doctoral degrees, the fast-moving nature of knowledge, internationalisation, the demands of funding bodies and employers... " *(p. 1).*

She also mentioned the untrained supervisors who normally supervise students the way they were self-supervised. These are among the challenges caused by the increasing access and the number of students in HE.

One of my informants, John, a teacher, explained:

"... In this university, a lecture can have more than 30 students to supervise, especially in undergraduate classes. The overloading practice poses difficulties to supervisors, especially when students are provided with an assignment because it is a huge responsibility for the teacher to read all students' work

critically". He continued: "*Even in group discussions without an assistant, a lecturer finds difficulty to facilitate all the groups in teaching. Most of the time, not all groups obtain an opportunity to share their work with others due to the limited time allocated for such a discussion and the number of groups in one seminar session. Likewise, the level of students' understanding varies widely to the extent of creating a challenge for the majority to learn from each other's input.*"

Indeed, supervisors face challenges dealing with many students and their diversities. Undoubtedly, the increased students population has been mentioned as one of many challenges facing universities faculties. However, John admits that students in a large, diverse class with many students may have the advantage where students and academics create a wide network.

The information presented by John aligns with what scholars; Stensaker et al. (2008), Van der Wende (2007, 2015) demonstrated when discussed about internationalisation in HE. They asserted that the rapid increased students population in HE, especially in the western and northern universities, has become a challenge in students learning and supervision. The scholars believed that this trend might favour the interest of the governments that focus on economic benefits while minimising the students' and academics' learning goals. Therefore, the practice of degree learning is different from the traditional era of HE.

Diverse Degrees and its Acquisition

Currently, there is an increased number of degree programs. Traditionally, few faculties and fields of studies were known for a degree. Thus, the traditional degrees were awarded in literature, theology, medicine, and a number (engineering and mathematics) (Simpson, 1983). As mentioned earlier, most HEIs have expanded the degree programmes to non-traditional fields such as arts, music, dance, nursing, and sports. Traditionally, these professional fields had no degree programmes, and their learning environment and structure were different from the traditional degree programs (Manathunga et al. (2007), Usher (2002), Wisker & Robinson (2015)). These pieces of evidence in unfamiliar degrees are discussed by Lee (2007) and Park (2007), who informed some benefits and challenges of providing diverse research degrees.

The diversity is both in the type and the process of obtaining a degree. The diversity is mainly observed in a doctoral degree where one can undertake a degree in the traditional programmes (literature, mathematics, laws, and medicine) or the newly established fields (dance arts, sports, and nurse). Besides, a candidate can also acquire a Ph.D. in traditional programmes by writing a thesis or by publications which is the modern way of acquiring a doctorate (Usher, 2002). Others prefer a Ph.D. by coursework where teaching is involved, and assignments are provided to the students through formative learning. Students have to produce pieces of academic papers apart from final thesis work. Moreover, students may acquire a Ph.D. by a project related to a specific field as it is in most professional doctorates (McAlpine & Amundsen (2016), Usher (2002)).

Private writing without supervision can also lead to a degree(UIO, 2021). A person can acquire a doctoral degree by private writing in many universities around the world. For example, in the Scandinavian countries, and Norway in particular: "a Dr. Philos is normally awarded to candidates who have published their work in the doctorate standard upon assessment and must conduct two official lectures and one public dialogue."(p. 1). Independent work without supervision is a procedure the University of Oslo stipulates to allow people to gain doctoral degrees from the normal recognized formal education system.

As well, the University of Auckland (UoA, 2021) stipulates:

"The university offers higher doctorates in Engineering (DEng), Laws (LLD), Literature (LittD), and Science (DSc)... to graduates or close affiliates of the University of Auckland who have published original work that has, over an extensive period, given them authoritative standing and international eminence in their respective field."(p.1).

Therefore, it is possible to acquire a doctoral degree without contact with a supervisor. For more information, one needs to read the universities web pages and contact the officials in charge of the discipline intended.

Indeed, the diversity of the type and the style of acquiring doctoral degrees have changed. Some of the practices have changed due to the knowledge economy and the authoritative nature of HE. For example, other HE levels, such as bachelor's and master's degrees, have also changed in type and way of acquiring them (Coleman, 2017). It has been observed that the diversities of degrees are among factors indicating that one structure or practice cannot "fit for all." The current alteration of practices is among the differences from the traditional HE practices.

Diverse Learning Agencies

Different learning agencies facilitate the open doors for diverse degrees and programmes. Current HE learning seems like an entrepreneur fashion show, attracting different views, learning styles, actors, and learning content. Students tend to meet with different learning facilitators with different backgrounds, qualities, and values. For example, individuals of all experiences are welcome to either learn or facilitate learning (Hillman, Tandberg, & Fryar, (2015), Kiley (2011a). Thus, the learning environment consists of different sellers and buyers, just as it is in any shopping centres, where all who desire to sell and buy operate the market.

Likewise, most learning programmes are displayed online, and students select and register themselves to the courses based on their interests and requirements. Most universities officials encourage students to attend relevant programmes through workshops and seminars for their learning and that, for research students, supervisors are no longer the only facilitators for student learning. There is an ongoing debate about multiple learning agencies and generic support provided to students in HE. For more information about the support, one may read the book by Carter (2014), where she discussed diverse ways, students learn. Many agencies are engaging in facilitating HE students learning today than ever before, online and in physical settings.

I had a conversation with Eshi, a tutor, who informed me how happy she was for the opportunity of teaching Ph.D. students. She asserted: *"I was very excited when I was appointed to teach Ph.D. students how to monitor long documents and use Microsoft word; I was very excited and worried at the same time. I thought the course coordinator was wrong, and maybe he would change his mind because such responsibility was not traditionally for a librarian like me. Furthermore, the teaching duty for Ph.D. students was for those with a Ph.D. or extended qualifications, not someone with a bachelor's degree like me.*

However, I have a long experience working as a secretary, and later, I worked as a student advisor. I studied some librarian courses at this university, which qualified me to work as a librarian and a tutor. Apart from that, I have supported many professors and lecturers with their writings, helping them organize their work and proofread their writings. I think the teachers whom I supported might be the ones who recommended my name to the Ph.D. course coordinator for me to work as a tutor. I am happy, and I do my work wholeheartedly; I also think one day I might undertake a master's and doctoral degree."

I agree with Eshi that in a traditional Ph.D., she could have difficulty obtaining such teaching assignments for students at the highest level of education. However, the focus on teachers' qualifications has changed from education level to the skills required by students. Therefore, the selection of learning agencies is diverse depending on the skills, competencies, and knowledge the agent possesses and can share. Indeed, learning agencies in the modern HE era have become different from traditional ones and may play different roles.

Revolution in Supervision Pedagogy

Supervision is a term that can be defined in diverse ways depending on the discipline and the task. For example, the concept of clinical supervision is different from educational supervision (Bernard, Goodyear (2005), (Grant (2005, 2008), Wisker (2005, 2010) Amundsen, & McAlpine (2009), Lee (2007)), although both may demonstrate leadership attributes of a person leading another or others. However, the discussion in this section will focus solely on educational supervision and specific HE. Supervision in HE is often linked to teaching and evaluation due to the historical background of teaching and assessment (Marzano, Frontier, & Livingston, 2011). Scholars such as Burke and Krey (2005), Marzano et al. (2011) provided an extensive historical background of supervision, which will not be repeated in this book.

However, in a nutshell, supervision started as inspection in the 1700s in the American school system. Marzano et al. (2011) asserted: that supervision (which changed from inspection) was a process of monitoring teacher's quality of instruction for employment purposes. Supervisors could positively or negatively recommend teachers' quality, and the comments could affect teachers' employment accordingly. Marzano et al. (Ibid) explained that supervisors had unlimited power over teachers' assessment in teaching skills, including the ability to mobilise students' efforts and involvement. The scholar demonstrated supervisory models and evolution from school inspection (fault detective) to supervision (supportive partnership). The system turned from instruction scrutinization and monitoring of teachers to cooperation and enhancing students' learning.

Conversely, supervision is still the instrument of quality assurance regardless of the level of education. Although the supervision priority has shifted from teachers' qualification evaluation to students' knowledge acquisition, supervision still informs the learning process and quality of teaching. Thus, supervision and leadership are inseparable; that is why Burke and Krey (2005) contended that; the idea of supervision refers to instructional leadership and inspection of the quality of teaching and learning. The scholars further described the weakness of school inspection, which focused on the judgmental nature and its tendency to "fault-finding" without guiding teachers for the quality of learning.

Others define supervision as a management task. For example, Lee (2007), Wisker & Robinson (2016) defined supervision of research students as a process of managing a research project and a student while encouraging the student to be an independent researcher. Lee & Green (2009) asserted that: the metaphor of 'super vision' means to enlighten a visualisation and provide revelation that brings an understanding to an area of expertise and communicates and meets the intended standards. Their perception aligns with what Halse and Malfroy (2010) emphasises: "... the supervisor provided oversight and guidance..." (p. 80). Wisker, Kiley, and Masika (2016) conceptualise supervision as a process of assisting students to attain the "threshold crossings or learning leaps" (p. 117) and being able to demonstrate research skills from problem discovery to the writing up and the assessment. Connell and Manathunga (2012) contended that: supervision is an advanced, complex, distinctive mode of teaching, individually structured, relational dependency, and difficulty functioning in a team. These definitions reflect the task aspects and reflect the diversity of tasks and the challenges in the supervision process.

Certainly, the learning structure in HE depends on, among others, students' supervision pedagogy. Supervisors facilitate students' learning through teaching, guidance, feedback through formal and casual interactions. In most institutions, especially where students are learning through a research project without course work (in the case of most master and doctoral degrees in some countries and institutions), supervisors play a crucial role in students' learning (Grant (2003, 2005a, 2005b), Lee (2007), Wisker (2005, 2012)). The supervisors link the institution and the students in many ways, especially in academic and social aspects. In addition, supervisors are supposed to provide students' assistance and ensure institutional and governmental policies.

Wisker (2005, 2012) indicated how students could benefit from good supervisors, especially if the student is researching within the area of supervisors' expertise. However, currently, practically, several supervisors are supervising students who are dealing with projects that are out of supervisors' expertise and even the areas they have inadequate knowledge. The situation can sometimes create a challenge and misunderstanding between the students and the supervisors, limiting the support students could receive. Wisker (ibid) suggested that supervisors who inform students what is expected of them earlier dissolve several challenges and simplify the supervision process.

Without a doubt, the idea of learning from the supervisor's guidance is essential for HE students in most universities (Bethany, Bell-Ellison & Robert, Dedrick (2008), Lesley Cooper et al. (2010)). However, if the supervisor neither understands the field nor provides field expertise, it might be challenging to inform students what is required apart from issues related to the research procedures. Likewise, when a supervisor does not know what students desire to research, the situation might force students to research in the area of the supervisor's expertise regardless of their preferences. This situation can become problematic, especially for students who have a specific area they desire to research.

For example, Colin, one of my informants, explained how his supervisor was unfamiliar with his research topic in the master's degree project. Every time the student discussed his project with the supervisor, the supervisor directed the student into another research topic of his interest. He wanted Colin to change the topic to suit his expertise, but it was hard because the student's project was one of the donor's interests to sponsor him. Besides, changing the topic could risk the student's scholarship, and therefore, he had to stand on his decision on the choice of the research topic. In such a situation, there was misunderstanding and dissatisfaction between the student and the supervisor for months. Finally, the supervisor stepped down from supervision when he failed to convince the student to change the research topic. However, it was difficult for the student to obtain another supervisor with the required expertise in his research topic.

Challenge in obtaining a perfect or even relevant supervisor is increased in HE. I heard from Calvin, another informant, about several students who dropped out simply because they were not heard or allowed to research the topic of their interest by their supervisors. The persuasion to change the research project occurred due to teachers' lack of knowledge of the field students desired to research. Unfortunately, some students reveal the weakness of their supervisors after their enrolment and in supervision meetings. I mentioned before people who have acquired two or more degrees of the same level for diverse reasons, including dissatisfaction with the already acquired degree. Indeed, it might be unfortunate to force students to research the area out of their interest for the sake of retaining them.

Another informant asserted that:

"One of the reasons I dropped out of HE was the idea of my supervisor to change my research topic and forced me to research the area in which I had no interest. I had to drop out, and I did not regret it because, after some months, I joined another university where I was supervised by a professor who is an expert in the topic of my interest. I have few months remain to graduate."

All in all, the challenge of finding qualified supervisors is growing. The diversity of students' research interests and multiple degree programmes may hinder some students from obtaining a supervisor with expert requested students.

The issue of supervision is fundamental and complex. Another informant, Mary, a student, suggested said: *"Some supervisors neglect the reality of subject expertise, and they tend to believe that by having a degree (the master's degree) they can automatically supervise bachelor research students in their project no matter the subject or field of interest. Others tend to think that having a Ph.D., Postdoc., or being a professor can legitimate supervising any graduate and postgraduate students regardless of their specialisation".*

Indeed, it is unclear how far one can go in supervising research students and the qualification essential for the task. However, the student demonstrated her evaluation and the significant challenges facing supervisors and students associated with supervisors' qualifications.

I am not an expert and do not intend to judge the practices, but I want to discuss the information I obtained from students and academics concerning supervision. The majority admitted that it is more effective learning when supervising students in the area of expertise than in the traditional era of HE. Although most institutions encourage academics and students to be multidisciplinary-oriented and supervisors are undertaking supervision programmes (Kiley (2011a), Underwood & Austin (2016)), we do not have to undermine the power of specialisation. No academic understands everything in every field, and that those focusing on a particular field tend to be resourceful to their learners and the field development.

Supervisors' Multiple Functions

Most institutions desire the MAN WHO KNOWS ALL. It might be a strategy of minimising the costs associated with retaining academics. Unfortunately, scholarly literature has informed the challenges associated with a mismatch of the supervisor and the field of expertise, the mismatch between the students and the supervisor as a person, and the disasters it may cause in learning (Grant (2008), Murphy (2009)). Although most supervisors are expected to be research experts, mastering the subject or the field knowledge and understanding the vital critical players in the field is equally important.

Likewise, supervisors' mastering of diverse disciplines from diverse backgrounds is a vital quality required today. Even though many institutions have introduced training programmes for supervisors (Eley & Jennings (2005), Kiley (2011a)), supervisors' qualifications associated with research and field are still essential. Indeed, most supervisors' programmes aim at empowering supervisors with supervising knowledge; still, the contents of most training programmes focus on supervisors/students' interactions. The programmes indicate the procedures to be followed in supervision, information students ought to receive, students, supervisors, institutions' expectations, and their roles (Halse (2011), Kiley (2011a)). However, this knowledge does not increase supervisors' specific subject/discipline or field expertise.

Indeed, supervisors' specialisation can lead to clear and meaningful support for students. It might be an advantage for students to be guided to the workshops and seminars related to the field when a supervisor is an expert in the same field (Lee, 2008). It is not my intention to write about the quality of a good supervisor in this book because scholars such as Wisker (2005, 2012), Grant (2005, 2008), Amundsen and MacAlpine (2009), and Halse (2011) have written on the same topic. Likewise, the scholars have discussed the characteristics, qualifications, and attributes a good supervisor should demonstrate, and the challenges HE teachers encounter today. They also indicated some supervisors' struggles with students in supervision and suggestions that can support those who desire to be good supervisors. The great emphasis is that the expertise of a supervisor should not be measured by how well a supervisor follows procedures in supervision, but the mastering of discipline and the research topic of students' interest.

In addition, many supervisors have different academic backgrounds and learning cultures from the students they supervise. These differences sometimes tend to be a stumbling block for students' learning and their cooperation in supervision in general (Grant, 2008). As a result, some students experience a damaging learning situation that becomes regrettable and unforgettable lifelong. For example, if the students and supervisors have no inclusive learning perspectives, are not integrated with multicultural ideas, and suppose they both have different cultures, their relationship may be problematic. Nevertheless, I cannot deny that some supervisors succeed in their supervision regardless of students' backgrounds, discipline, interests, research topic, and other factors. However, one may think that these successful supervisors are good at discussing sensitive issues with their students, such as culture, values, and expectations. They also manage to formulate common ground for their practices before engaging in supervision.

Ethical observation in supervision is another vital aspect to consider. The literature has shown different situations where supervision turns into a destructive pedagogy. Sometimes, a slave and a master like a relationship (Grant, 2008) where students' ideas, culture, skills, and wellbeing are not valued. Some supervisors tend to be gods and goddesses for students (as discussed earlier), and students have to worship them and follow carefully the instructions provided by these supervisors. In other cases, if the students violate the obedience, they may suffer neglect and abandonment from their supervisors. Others face challenges associated with their demographic and historical background (Kidman, Manathunga, & Cornforth (2017), Manathunga, Guilherme, & Dietz (2017)). Therefore, there are conflicting perceptions on the relationship supervisors should demonstrate in supervision. Some think supervisors need to be more responsible in creating a conducive supervision environment with their students rather than exercising their power, while others believe both students and supervisors are equally responsible. Thus, there are changes in the current role of HE supervisors from the traditional era, and that a supervisor is no longer the only supporting agent for students to succeed. However, even though students receive support from various learning agencies, supervisors' tasks have not been reduced; instead, they perform diverse duties.

Supervisor as a "Superman"

Currently, supervisors have different tasks to perform. The workload depends on the nature of the project. Other factors that determine the supervisor's task are relationships with the student, the student's academic capabilities, time allocated for supervision, and the stage a research student has achieved. Some scholars such as Wisker et al. (2004), Xu and Grant (2017), Lee (2008), Chiappetta-Swanson and Watt (2011) explained different phases and the involvement of a supervisor and the vital art of knowing when to lead the students and when to let students lead the learning and the supervision. Nevertheless, in this modern era of HE, supervisor's responsibilities have turned to be many and vary from one student to the other, one department and the rest, institution and others. Most supervisors are expected to deal with diverse aspects of students' academic, social, personal well-being and policy issues (Wisker et al., 2016). Even with the Bologna agreement of European countries (Van der Wende (2007, 2015) of standardising higher education practices, supervisors' roles are still diverse and cannot be uniform to all students.

Chiappetta-Swanson and Watt (2011) described the role of a supervisor to support students as: "a coach, mentor, guide model, and manager" (p.5) aiming at preparing a candidate for employment. Likewise, Lee (2005) asserted that; the major task of a supervisor is to direct and empower students to follow the research procedures and standards required and support students in writing. These scholars theorise the role of a supervisor in different perspectives and that their conceptualisation varies as the supervision tasks and style do.

For example, in Figure 3, an attempt is made to point out a supervisor's responsibilities in supervision. The grouping is not ranked based on the importance of the role neither limited to the title provided; instead, it is written randomly to simplify the understanding of the immediate task associated with the task title.

As a Leader
Representative
Vision
Purpose
Values
Strategies
Engangement
Empowerment
Evaluate

As a Guider
Consult
Negotiator
Gatekeeper
Assesser
Superstar
Oversight
Strategize
Advice

As a Researcher
Support student in;
constructing a
research
Research topic
Questions
Methods
Methodology
Analysis
Ethics

Supervisor's
Responsibilities

As a Friend
Socialization
Advice
Listener
Assist
Inform
Encourage
Community
Network

As a Mentor
Trust
Facilitate
Modelling
Dialogue
Support
Emotional
Motivate

As a Teacher
Instruct
Feedback
References
Regulations
Communicate
Presentation
Writing

Figure 3. The Expected Roles of a Supervisor

As indicated, figure three summarize the roles of a supervisor. Indeed, supervisors in higher education are like Superman. For example, a supervisor is expected to be the caretaker of every aspect of students' learning to judge the outcomes. I do not wish to repeat them in this paragraph; however, I study the figure and observe the roles and comprehend that they may differ from one department to another, institution to others, and country to another. As a student, do not expect much from supervisors even though their tasks may be infinitive. Instead, you ought to check out the contextual roles of supervisors from the beginning to avoid unrealistic expectations. Practicing evaluation of supervisors' responsibilities will save much time most students use for resolving misunderstandings in supervision.

For instance, Lee (2007) mentioned a supervisor being a "porter, organizer, network" and even "a family doctor" (p. 687) and an owner of the results. However, not all supervisors perform these duties, and the dangerous part of regarding a supervisor as a Superman is like that expressed by Lee (ibid) that "… the supervisor can choose which gates to open, particularly in the early stages …" (p.687) and that can be either an advantage or disadvantage for the student. The metaphors provided by Lee of gate opening indicate the vital position and power of a supervisor. Indeed, I cannot emphasise enough how vital the supervisors are in research students' learning success; THEY ARE VERY IMPORTANT!

A piece of advice

I think students' values and beliefs need to be taken seriously in supervision. If neglected by a supervisor, it might affect the creativity and curiosity required of students. Factors like religion, clothing, race and historical oppression related to race and religious background should be discussed openly when necessary. Pretending to have no differences in human thinking, histories, and cultural practices is like keeping an explosive chemical object on hold. The relationship in supervision is one of the major issues that lead to students' success or failure in their studies. So, you have to observe your contact with your supervisor and keep it open and professional.

The topic of supervision in HE is worthy of time and debate for more clarifications. One should check with the supervisor's expertise and availability before enrolment. After enrolment, if you think the supervisor is not fulfilling your needs, it is better to report immediately. If the complaint does not lead to appropriate supervision and fair judgment, you must inform the university officials about your thinking and feelings. I suggest students be active in their learning and attempt by all means to express their expectations. Indeed, they may "drop out" when they see their needs and anticipations are not supervisors' priorities even after discussion. To be honest, it is not worth wasting time and money to please institution officials and supervisors.

Remember, all is business, so demand good service, and refuse to waste your savings.

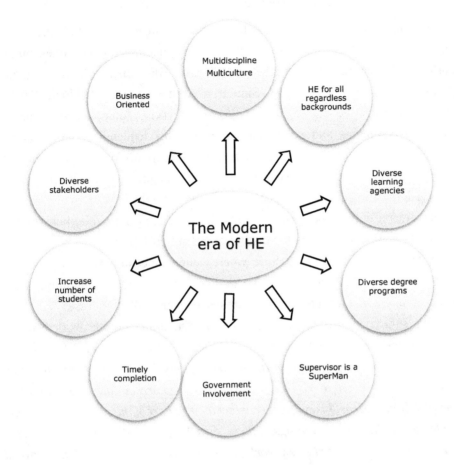

Figure 4. The Current Nature of Higher Education

As indicated in the figure, higher education in the modern era is business-oriented, and whoever affords the service financially and meets other requirements can access it regardless of his background. Furthermore, different learning agencies and stakeholders have involved even unprofessional teachers facilitate learning due to the increased number of students and the expansion of degree types. Likewise, most governments are the main financial donors and policymaking organs requiring students to complete their degrees quickly. In this case, the work of supervisors has become complex, and they work as a superman in a multicultural environment.

Who is Affected by the Changes?

Although most changes in HE learning are said to affect students, some supervisors are not satisfied with the changes they encounter either. For example, Carter and Kumar (2017) stated their concern over HE students who often ignore feedback from their supervisors. Similarly, Amundsen and McAlpine (2009) revealed a narrative conversation where a supervisor complained of being ignored by students and not taken seriously. This tendency of supervisors' feeling ignored may be rooted in the divergence perceptions between the students and the supervisors. Indeed, such feelings and thoughts may be destructive in supervision if not discussed openly. Again, this might be caused by, among others, diverse cultural perspectives and values or even gender roles between the supervisor and the student (Manathunga et al., 2017). For example, some students may come from a culture where gender and authority are observed differently from the teachers' perspective and the learning community. Other students may come from a culture where teachers are still "goddesses."

One supervisor, Andrew, complained about, doing double work because most students do not understand his feedback. He informed: *"When some students obtain my feedback on their writing, instead of correcting the part where I asked them to restructure, rewrite, or correct, they tend to write completely new ideas. Likewise, if I correct a large part of their work and provide feedback in their new writings, others rewrite yet another new work. This rewriting business leads to new work all the time rather than marching forward with the writing. It is very frustrating, and I do not know how to stop this kind of behavior because my conversation with some of these students indicates they understand the instruction, but their actions provide a different message."* The supervisor described this with disappointment, and this was about postgraduate students' writings. Although the supervisor did not explain the cause of the misunderstandings, I cannot avoid thinking that the language of instruction may be the main obstacle. There are other reasons, such as unclear instruction from the supervisor, lack of passion on a specific topic from students, but mainly language is one of the challenges that can bring the challenge the supervisors described. Students' misunderstandings of the supervisors' instructions are among the confusions that partners experience in supervision.

In another study by Amundsen and McAlpine, the policy of timely completion affected supervision. Most supervisors articulated their experiences of struggling with many students and the limited time required to complete their studies (Lee, 2007). Time limit, especially for master's and doctoral students, affects supervision negatively due to the pressure involved in meeting different deadlines required of them. In addition, the pressure from the institutions' administrators that mainly originated from the government often creates a stressful learning environment. The explanation aligns with what Lee (Ibid) communicated in her article "Developing effective supervision." She asserted that: the time pressure, misunderstanding of viewpoints, language, cultural differences, and the number of students to supervise are among the challenges that supervisors encounter in HE's teaching role.

Another group that is affected by the changes in HE is family. Families always have something to sacrifice when a member joins HE. For example, most families have to borrow money from different sources to support their members to join HE. Such practice for most families is perceived as an investment expecting a return in the future. However, even if they do not support their member financially, families encounter several challenges for the education of their members. One informant, Adela, described how she left two teenagers and headed for a doctoral degree.

She asserted: *"In fact, not many people understand the sacrifice required for the acquisition of a Ph.D. I desired to join HE for a doctoral degree. But since my children were small, I hesitated because there was no one I could trust to take care of them. My mother had my siblings to care for and other businesses that kept her very busy. My husband had a demanding job, and he did not support my ideas of Ph.D. studies at that moment. So, ... when my sons turned seventeen and twenty, I thought nothing could hinder me from acquiring the degree I desired. I left my sons with their daddy and headed for the education, knowing that they were grown up enough to make their lives the way they desired. I was lucky because they focused on their education, and their father reduced several working hours to follow them up. After my graduation, they had turned twenty-one and twenty-five, and both had hooked themselves to girlfriends. Indeed, I needed their company, but they were as busy as I were, and I seemed strange to them. I regret and feel that I missed part of their lives which I will never get back."*

Indeed, people who join HE, whether single, married, with children or no children, sacrifice part of their life or the life of their loved one. Some of them encounter challenges and think it was bad timing, they could wait, or they could learn earlier, and so on. However, the truth is that there is no suitable time for study, but the one individual creates and when one is motivated. Therefore, all the time, whether early or later, there are some sacrifices related to attaining a degree.

Honestly, the family members need awareness of the sacrifices and resources required by a family member for a degree. The evaluation of whether the person will obtain the support required should also be considered. The breakage of families due to education often happens, especially if no adequate information and preparation were involved. Most of us agree that education is a fundamental aspect of empowerment for families. However, empowerment through education needs a good foundation of information to support participants in making wise decisions. Women and other marginalized groups need crucial and careful planning for their inclusion to be beneficial and sustainable for families.

Understandably, it might be difficult for an individual to prepare for every corner of his life when undertaking a degree. However, having information about other people's experiences and the consequences their desire brought to their families can prepare them adequately. Indeed, studying in higher education should not be a game-like project where the participants receive and obey the command: ON YOUR MARKS, GET READY, GO. Therefore, joining HE should not be *OBTAINING FINANCE, GETS READY, AND JOIN.* Somewhat different issues are involved, including folks and other resources before deciding to join up HE studies. For example, someone must plan for short-term and long-term strategies and foresee the challenges, needs, and successes that might happen in the process by examining several aspects of his life beyond studies.

Therefore, I believe you have acquired information about the changes in HE learning that can support you in evaluating your situation and measure your motivation to head for a degree. You have also read other people's experiences and reactions to HE changes and the debates surrounding the learning practices. You may be scared and wonder why people should sacrifice so much for HE and what students learn. Therefore, I will discuss learning in HE in the following chapter. First, however, there are some questions that you need to consider as a summary in this chapter.

Self-Reflection

What changes have you observed in HE before reading this book?

Do you have the same thoughts you had before reading about the changes in HE?

Do you think HE for all is a good idea? In which way?

What are the effects of access to HE in the north and west countries to governments from south and east?

Do you think it is a good idea to have diverse learning agencies in HE? Debate on this.

What are your perspectives about the knowledge economy?

What do you think HE stakeholders in your country demand?

Do you think the increasing number of students is the major reason for all other changes? How?

What do you think institutions managements must do to enhance students' supervision?

What are the roles of a supervisor in your country and institution?

What are the advantages and disadvantages for a supervisor to have multiple responsibilities?

Are there other changes that you have observed in HE in your context? Mention them.

Chapter V
Theorising Higher Education Learning

There is an extensive range of theoretical concepts applicable to learning in HE. Learning has diverse definitions and theories based on individual objectives, preferences, and perceptions (Barron, Hebets, Cleland, Fitzpatrick, Hauber, & Stevens (2015), Washburne (1936)). People's definitions of learning and acknowledging who has acquired knowledge vary depending on the learner's behavior and the assessors' expectations. Indeed, people are assumed to join HE to learn new concepts or modify and upgrade the already known information. Thus, people theorise learned people based on what they believe to be the purpose of the learning. So, there are different perspectives to consider when theorising learning and even when defining it. The term learning has never had one definition neither theory.

Therefore, learning can be theorised based on the learners' perceptions and performance. Therefore, learning outcomes do not necessarily mean the grades the learner obtained from the formative and summative evaluations conducted by others, but the outcomes observed in her ability to communicate the knowledge and solve problems. In addition, the satisfaction learner acquires by meeting her expectations can inform the extent to which she has learned. However, the fundamental aspects of learning are observed practically in the person's reactions, actions, and capability to cooperate with others. Learning, however, can be categorised in different levels in linear or hierarchical as identified by Bloom's learning taxonomy. In this section, the main objective is not to define learning but to discuss multiple learning theories that can support you in formulating the definition of learning.

Behaviourist Learning Perspectives

Different psychologists conduct various attempts to examine what learning is and how it takes place. For example, behaviourists such as Skinner, Pavlov, and Watson demonstrated that learning is a change of behaviour (Evans, Richard I (Richard Isadore) & Skinner, 1964) and occurs when a learner interacts with learning content in a particular environment through reinforcement. The instructor controls this interaction and evaluates whether the learner has attained the learning goals. Evans, Richard, and Skinner (Ibid) argued that: *"Skinner discovered that* behavior *which operates in a* particular *environment is caused or controlled, not by a free learner's intrinsic motivation, but by external consequences or effects received or aroused from the surrounding environment."* (Evans, Richard & Skinner (1964) p. 5.

Applying this concept of learning in HE indicates that the instructor determines the kind of learning activities and outcomes desired for students' behavioural change. It means the supervisors control the learning environment, the learner, and the stimulus to create or regulate the behavior. Besides, upon demonstrating the instructor's desired behaviour, the learner is rewarded for strengthening his reactions. Likewise, negative reinforcement applies when a learner demonstrates the undesired behaviour to weaken it. As a result, the positive reinforcement promotes repetition, while the negative reinforcement hinders its recurrence. According to behaviourists, the repetitions of learners' actions and the positive reinforcement are the essences of learners' acquisition of new behavior, which leads to a permanent change and, hence learning.

Undeniably, the behaviourist definition of learning often objectifies learners and makes them the recipients of the commands from the instructors (Light & Evans, 2018). For example, Bandura (1977) observed the consequences of positive and negative reinforcement in learning and its effect on behavior change. He described learning as an epistemological understanding and ontological change that can be recognized by observing a learner's behaviour. When the desired character is executed repeatedly and automatically, it indicates a permanent change in learners' behaviour. The change may occur even when it is against learners' desire to cope with the control instructors impose through reinforcement.

Therefore, theorising learning using behaviourist concepts might not provide a whole picture of learning and how it occurs in HE. Yes, sometimes learning in HE can be passive for the learners, primarily when the teaching occurs in a lecture form where students listen to their teachers with a little contribution. For example, sometimes teachers provide a lecturer on a new topic for forty minutes or hours without interruptions and without accommodating questions. Unfortunately, in most such lectures, students may be asked to preserve their questions (if any), and they may ask at the end of a long lecture. Often, students who do not write their questions progressively tend to forget what they desired to ask at the end of the lecture, and hence no questions. In such a situation, students become recipients and passive learners, and sometimes if the teacher will provide them with an assignment on the topic, they have to respond the way the teacher desire.

Likewise, most of the time, learners' in HE do not have adequate intrinsic motivation, neither the appropriate rewards required to enhance the acquisition of the required behaviour. If we refer to why people join HE, you may realize that some join for purposes other than knowledge and skills, and they may have low intrinsic motivation. Such students who learn by lecturers depend on the appropriate rewards from their learning agencies to enhance the acquisition of the required behaviour. Others join their teachers' research projects, and they sometimes depend on the process, and strategies teachers have formulated for the project and sometimes become passive. Therefore, if people consider learning in HE using only the behaviourists' perspectives, they will be disappointed because students are no longer the recipients of teachers' perspectives without questioning. Besides, learners' behavioural change can result from other factors, not necessarily the teacher's or other learning agencies' control (Barron et al., 2015). Likewise, learners in HEIs are encouraged to be active participants, and they are supposed to examine the practices that need modification or change critically. Thus, they are expected to create new knowledge and share it with others, which rarely can happen passively.

A Catalyst for Better Communication

Indeed, an individual's communication tends to indicate his learning. Learning can be theorised based on the learner's communication with subjects and objects around him. Students in HE, interact with diverse subjects such as learning agencies that construct their communication ability. They learn by observing how others are communicating, and they enhance their contact with them. However, not all students have adequate communication skills, but those who have realised the need and benefits of correct interaction have learned and developed such skills. Certainly, communication includes mastering the language (Boyle, Carpenter & Mahoney, 2017) and the choice of words. The learned person needs to demonstrate good interaction by understanding when to communicate and convey the correct information. Moreover, the person should learn the strategies applied to communicate correctly and the targeted people for the message.

Therefore, what the learners learn, should enhance their interaction and improve their communication. Most HEIs support students in acquiring new communication strategies that better reflect their thinking, actions, and reactions towards diverse issues. Refer to the story of graduates and farmers by Simpson (1983), where he communicated his knowledge to the right people at the right time.

Change of Performance

Learning is a change of performance. People learn to acquire knowledge that modifies their presentation, whether they like it or not. For instance, some people perform their duties differently after acquiring new knowledge, even if sometimes they are unconscious of their actions. Maybe you have heard people who knew someone from before and the person join HE, and they wonder what has happened to the person by his actions. I can share a story about my friend Mary, a trendy girl in high school. The first qualification was that she used to speak directly to aggressive boys telling them to stop bullying without fear. Those days of my high school, there were some boys who most girls were afraid of, but Mary was like the saviour of other girls. She was aggressive and fond of confrontations and sometimes fought with boys who expressed bullying behavior in the class. Her confident behaviour scared most boys and other people around her, and she was regarded as an unapproachable person.

After high school, Mary joined HE, where she studies and successfully graduated. After that, she was employed in a state organisation as a social worker. Many people, who knew her, started noticing the changes in her behaviour through performance. She became a good listener, tolerant, and a humble person compared to how she acted before joining HE. The realisation came out later that Mary studied sociology in HE, and she came across many theories related to social behaviour and human relations that changed her mindset. The learning contents and her willingness to critically comply with the learned information created her new perspectives and behaviour. She did not tell people what she learned or discuss the theories, but her presentation showed her successful learning.

According to the earlier mentioned psychologists, learning successfulness is associated with learners' behavioural change, not grades. Indeed, performance speaks louder than grades, and it means one might have good grades in his examinations but not necessarily the indication that the person has learned. People are used to ask someone's grades with little attention to performance, but within a short time, they realise the level of the individual's learning by his performance. The philosophy of performance responds to the question many people used to ask or joke about concerning graduates. Some wonder why some graduates with excellent grades are not as qualified in their performance in the job market as indicated on their certificates. The response is that learning is not measured by acquiring good grades but by the learners' knowledge and skills. Although the grading system in formal education forces people to believe grades can measure the level of learning and individual's ability, it is not an issue of taking for granted.

Sometimes, when people graduate, their qualifications are realised by old friends quicker than anybody else. Graduates who have learned successfully may be noticed and may no longer have the type of performance they used to have with friends or act the same way as before. The majority of observers tend to think their graduate friends are boasting or have some problems, especially those who do not know much about learning and its changes. Some people tend to have difficulty acknowledging that the graduates' actions are associated with the learning that has taken place and the changes in their performance (Keefer (2015), Kiley & Wisker (2010)).

If a leaner's performance has not changed, learning has not taken place the way it ought to be. Therefore, people who desire to join HE must understand that folks are expecting their learning to be practical through their presentation, and in this case, better performances. I am afraid that formal education examiners will stop grading people and let their performance in real-life talk for them. However, changing the grading system requires strategies and preparations that HE practitioners and other stakeholders must agree upon.

Change of Perspectives

It is amazing how people's perceptions may change after learning. I have to tell this story of one lady, Jamaima, who had worked for a particular company for more than eight years before joining HE. She was performing very well in the job and was one of the most likable persons in the company. She went for a degree, and after graduation, she returned to her former position as a secretary, receiving and registering clients' application forms and distributing cases to other people in the company. The co-workers were assigned to deal with the cases and responded to the clients accordingly. Jamaima, in her return from HE, had different observations of the existing practices in her company, although she had practiced the same procedure for almost nine years. She found the practices were ineffective and caused resource wastage. She believed she could support the company with her knowledge better if she could be in a decision-making position. She desired to make a little change, which could free her from her current position, and that client could send their applications and complaints directly to her colleagues who were dealing with such cases without her receiving them and sending them over. She shared her idea with her immediate leader, expecting to be listened to, and probably implementing her suggestion could occur.

Her boss had a different perspective that conflicted with Jamaima's. He perceived her as a person who was seeking attention and not willing to work. She was regarded as a threat to her boss and an incompetent person unwilling to receive instructions like others. Then, Jamaica's boss started to have adverse reactions and feelings about her behaviour changes and the tendency to question different company officials' practices. The employee's change created some tensions and misunderstandings between the two. Jamaima changed from a likable person to a rebellious one who was seeking trouble. The situation became unpleasant to the extent of forcing the female employee to seek a job somewhere else.

Indeed, Jamaima, obtained another job in another company dealing with a similar kind of service to people. In the new company, the leaders were good listeners, and Jamaima's ideas related to providing effective services were received positively. The company quickly implemented Jamaima's suggestions about digital application forms and direct connection between the clients and the advisors as a new way of communication. The direct contact with advisors eliminated secretarial work of receiving and distributing work to advisors. As a result, the company reduced the number of workers and became the first to digitalise their service for effective and quick service. They even managed to solve the problem of keeping records because all advisors remained with the list of the customers they had attended and the type of service provided. Indeed, the company flourished due to the idea from Jamaima and the perspectives and effort they put into it.

Currently, almost all companies and organisations in most countries prefer digital applications. Moreover, the communication with customers goes directly to the people who can deal with the cases on hand without a go-between (secretary), something Jamaima desired to introduce in the previous company. Jamaima obtained the idea after critical thinking of how well she could utilize her time and knowledge for better and effective production. The change of mindset for both Jamaima and the new company's officials is one of the indicators demonstrating learning. Jamaima had learned, and the new company officials were ready to learn and successfully implemented the constructive idea for their benefit.

Sometimes, HE learning can cause a sense of insecurity to people around a graduate. It is not surprising for two sides (the graduate and the non-graduate) in the working place to conflict, especially when both lack an integrated mindset. One should remember that the main reason for misunderstandings might be that one has gained critical thinking ability and the other has not, or one has an integrated mind-set and the other has not. Sometimes, both parties may have critical thinking ability, but are incompatible and cannot communicate their differences, but other reasons might be the reason. For example, when assigned to do something, let us say, two people, one might receive the instruction and implement it theologically without critical thinking, while the other might require time to think critically about the instruction before the implementation. As a result, the evaluator of these two mindsets might have different opinions about the effectiveness of the pair.

Understand the concept of critical thinking, I do not mean graduates are more critical thinkers or effective workforce than others, but I want to establish how important it is for people to theorize learning from broad perspectives. Besides, some people who do not have a degree sometimes become offended by graduates. They think they disregard knowledge from others, and sometimes, their thinking creates behaviour that hinders them from cooperating. For example, I have experienced that sometimes, when a leader lacks a degree and is not the employer or owner of the organization, it can be a disaster working with graduates, and they sometimes work to demonstrate the weaknesses of graduates than cooperation. As a result, the graduates may be placed where they cannot function and contribute to their highest, and instead of their knowledge being utilized and appreciated, it becomes wastage. So, they do not demonstrate their ability, and their behavioural change is not recognized rather are feared and regarded threats to others. So, yes, learning can be acknowledged by the change of ones' behaviour, and if there is no change of behaviour observed, people think that the person has not learned. Therefore, the learned person has to create an environment to demonstrate the change of behaviour or should obtain the position to

Critical Thinking

Learning is an active process of acquiring knowledge. If you are a person who desires to receive and follow instructions without critical thinking, you might perceive learning in HE as a complex process. Students need to have self-initiative, self-management, and intrinsic motivation (Ryan & Deci, 2000). The learners ought to understand what's required of them, what they anticipate, and how to achieve the desired outcomes. For example, the learners may receive instructions or directions on what to do from the learning agencies (refer behaviourists), but they should be able to make independent decisions on whether the directions or instructions provided meets their requirements and will lead to the attainment of their learning goals. The learners will have to evaluate the directives critically to bring the best results even beyond the expected. Indeed, learners in HE must be critical and independent in decision-making rather than following the instruction robotically. Students are expected to be curious and active in seeking knowledge and skills required for problem-solving.

Ryan and Deci (2000) asserted:

"The fullest representations of humanity show people to be curious, vital[ity], and self-motivated. At their best, they are agents and inspired, striving to learn, extend themselves; master new skills, and apply their talents responsibly. That most people show considerable effort, agency, and commitment in their lives *appears* to be more normative than exceptional, suggesting some very positive and persistent features of human nature."

Therefore, as a learner in HE, you are expected to practice what Ryan and Deci described, the human nature of demonstrating curiosity by criticising and modifying the instructions. Doing so will create better and new knowledge beyond expectations and is a characteristic of a learned person. Although there are some challenges to attain critical thinking and demonstrate the level of ability required, evidence illustrates that most graduates have acquired vital qualifications (Mowbray & Halse, 2010). The scholars indicated that quality learning is different between academic and non-academics, but most students comprehend their knowledge acquisition even though other people may have different perspectives. It is evidence that learning in HE has diverse definitions based on stakeholder perspectives and the area that interested them. However, most people believe that upon graduation, a student must have acquired critical and independent thinking.

Though there is no objective measure applied to the evaluation of graduates' critical thinking, there are some qualities expected of graduates as a sign of reaching the critical intellectual mind-set. Most universities focus on the development of creativity and some characteristics that indicate students' learning trajectories. Some stipulate consequential series of conceptualizations standards through which students should attain. Others undertake both formative and summative evaluation and assign grades as a sign of students' attainment of the expected learning goal (Graff, Russell, & Stegbauer, 2007). Nevertheless, most academics tend to realise when students have crossed the level of understanding required by demonstrating critical thinking on diverse issues. Most academics call "threshold crossing" is an example of the transformation observed in students' performance when learning occurs (Kiley & Wisker, 2010). Thus, learning is the process of attaining cognitive transformation that can be recognised when students understand what was difficult to be understood before.

The ability to think critically is an important goal in HE. Students learn how to scrutinise and criticise the literature and the practices in their field to transform Anderson & Caldwell (2017). For example, I discussed HE changes from traditional practices to the modern era in the previous chapter. The changes are evidence of the transformation originating from the critical thinking of some higher education stakeholders. Most of the changes in education from kindergarten to university, are the results of people's critical thinking. Indeed, some are observant of gaps in the system and practitioners, and they fill the gaps with knowledge. Therefore, the critical thinking minds are fundamental and the foundation of all human development and revolutions in education and other sectors.

According to Simpson (1983), the primary task of traditional HE was to produce critical thinkers who change their thoughts to knowledge and skills and labourers for societal development. This belief still exists in the modern era of

HE, where scholars Kiley & Wisker (2010), Wisker (2012), and Wisker & Robinson (2015, 2016) indicated the learning expectations and wellbeing of graduates and supervisors. Indeed, the focus is to empower students with knowledge that will support them to create critical thinking and intensify their ability to cooperate with supervisors and solve diverse problems independently.

Hierarchical Activities

Similarly, Bloom's taxonomy contends that learning is hierarchical task performance. He pointed out that learning occurs gradually depending on the activities learners are ready to perform. He asserted that learning is a systematic intellectual development, which follows a specific hierarchical framework (Weigel & Bonica, 2014). According to Bloom's taxonomy, learning occurs through two levels; a lower level where a learner can remember, understand and apply the knowledge, and the higher level where a learner analyse, evaluate, and create knowledge (Anderson & Krathwohl (2001), Krathwohl (2002), Weigel & Bonica (2014)).

The taxonomy illustrates that the attainment of higher levels of learning depends on the mastering of the lower levels. The hierarchy means the successful learning of, as an example, primary and secondary school facilitate learning in HE. Therefore, activities performed at lower levels of learning are not less valuable, but they are the necessary foundation for the activities undertaken at a higher level. The difference is that the activities performed at higher levels of learning demand higher intellectual capabilities that evaluate the existing knowledge and modify or create a new one. This concept of categorising learning based on the learners' activities is vital for the evaluation of appropriate activities and learner's capabilities. The taxonomy can also be applied in constructing learning, evaluating the outcome, and assigning tasks to people in the job market.

Therefore, theorising learning through activities and learners' functionality is beneficial for economic purposes. When people operate in their position and learning level, they tend to be more productive than the opposite. However, some employers are not aware of Bloom's taxonomy, and if they were, they could save many resources. Indeed, Bloom's taxonomy may support employers in predicting the kind of knowledge and skills expected of the employee based on their learning level. Without a doubt, the understanding could support employers in hiring people and positioning them correctly according to their expertise and skills. For instance, if an employer is looking for a person who can remember things, arrange, or rearrange things, in one way or the other, they do not need to look for a graduate to perform the task. Positioning a graduate to perform such duties will be a waste of resources because such tasks are among the activities that people with lower levels of education can undertake.

Indeed, little is known about the relationship between learning and task performance. In a conference with some employers, I remember we discussed the skills required in the job market. These employers complained about the incompetence of some graduates who were working in their companies. During the tea/coffee break, I had an opportunity to exchange some words with few employers where I questioned their views concerning their graduates' employees. My question to them was, "what kind of tasks the unqualified graduates had in their workplace?". Based on their responses, I found that almost all employers had misplaced their graduate staff.

Undeniably, people need to comprehend that learning is a hierarchical conscientisation that facilitates particular abilities. Most of these company leaders, after our discussion, realised that they did not require graduates in some of the positions where they employed them. The misplacement might be one of the reasons the graduates' performances were not satisfactory and were unsuccessful. The graduates were like fish out of water, forced to swim on land, where they could not demonstrate their capability. The experience with employers taught me that the learned person must perform appropriate duties for learning outcomes to be appreciated. Graduates should be assigned tasks that require them to apply their critical thinking and knowledge to be productive; otherwise, hiring them in positions that requires a low level of learning outcomes may hinder them from being productive. The situation may even disqualify graduates, regardless of competencies and skills they have probably acquired. Therefore, learning is hierarchical task-oriented, where individuals utilize the knowledge and skills to solve problems based on their learning level; however, the ability is not an educational level dependency, but one's learned capacity.

Increased Learner's Capability

Almost all learning focuses on the increased learners' ability to perform a task. The abilities may differ and that learning in HE discourages judgmental evaluation learners' capability. For example, as a student, you are argued to be critical, defend what you mean is correct or meaningful, and convince other people to accept your perspectives. The ultimate goal of learning in HE is to support a learner to increase capability in arguments, to be able to convince correctly, to persuade people to take his advice, and to welcome input to your ideas. It is not to force people to accept your ideas but to support them to see the values of the ideas and be willing to apply them in policy implementation or other problem-solving responsibilities.

Refer to the story I provided earlier, in which Simpson (1983) discussed concerning a graduate who informed farmers about the significance of chemicals in farming by his research findings through a lecture. The graduate's idea resulted in the establishment of a chemical factory. The lecturer to farmers was a way the graduate demonstrated his learning and convinced investors to invest by establishing a chemical factory. It means that HEIs provide helps to students to learn and acquire appropriate and useful knowledge that supports the graduates in increasing their performances. Such conceptualisation in creating and enhancing the learners' ability is still observed, expected, and operates in HE learning today (Palmer, 2012). The graduate in question, had learned and as a result the learning increased his performance.

The application of knowledge is vivid in most cases. For instance, if a student had a problem using Microsoft Word, he is expected to solve this problem in different situations after learning how to use the programme. So, if he has learned, he will not experience the same problem, and if the problem occurs, he will be able to solve it and even support others with the knowledge. Therefore, the practical utilization of information indicates competence the learner acquires as a result of learning. Therefore, learning is not merely changing behaviour philosophically or demonstrating critical thinking but the tool to increase learners' ability to understand, modify the situation, and solve the problems.

Learning is Task-Oriented

Observing learning through the task a learner can perform should be the main focus. Indeed, HE stakeholders need to understand some learning principles (Weigel & Bonica, 2014) to better utilise employees' skills and competencies. For example, there are differences in knowledge and skills required for service provision and production. If employers need someone who can formulate a project, monitor it, evaluate it, and write a report, they probably need a graduate. The task provided to graduates may determine their capability in problem-solving and an indicator of whether learning has taken place or not. As I mentioned earlier, this assessment is vital in the job market yet unknown to many organisations and people who deal with employment.

Refer to the employers in the conference I mentioned earlier, most employers had hired graduates to perform tasks that non-graduates could accomplish. At the same time, they wondered why the graduates were not competent or productive. One of the graduates I shared these experiences with Angela contended: *"Of course, a graduate who accepts to work for a position that does not require his knowledge or skills he might use most of his time looking for a better job and not performing in his current job. The graduate's mind will be uncertain all the time, expecting to quit anytime upon obtaining a better job. Often, they might have problems concentrating and focusing completely on the job, and due to this behavior, they are regarded as unproductive. Most graduates may be competent, but they do not fully apply their time on the job; they normally have divided minds until they get jobs requiring their qualifications. I also believe the graduates who accept to work in such lower positions are probably doing that for money, not for passion."*

Based on this explanation, I am convinced that if a person graduated successfully from an accredited higher education institution, he should have acquired multiple qualifications. The graduates themselves must acknowledge the qualifications they have acquired and the tasks they can perform well in the job market that requires their qualifications. I guess people complaining about the graduate's incompetence should re-examine the task expected of the graduates. The task of remembering information does not suit the graduates neither disqualify them. HE stakeholders need to discuss and understand the skills and competencies expected of graduates for their placement. Stakeholders must be aware of the tasks performed at different levels of learning to save the resources and time currently wasted by misplacing graduate employees. Regardless of economic crisis or pandemics, graduate experts should not be undermined but comprehended, enhanced, and utilised.

I mention that remembering is not the main task for graduates. It does not mean the graduates do not require to remember information. No, but importantly they need to understand how and where to obtain the updated information and utilise it in problem-solving. When dealing with issues or solving a problem, their primary focus is not how to retrieve the information but understanding the issue and solve the situation at hand is the most valuable. Therefore, not remembering yesterday's information should not disqualify graduates because they aim at bigger goals of creating new information, knowledge, transfer and store the information than remembering it (Anderson et al., 2001; Weigel & Bonica, 2014). This notion indicates that information can be changed and created by graduates based on the requirements.

I do not want to discuss misunderstandings between graduates and employers due to its disposition. But, unfortunately, it happens almost in every organisation, significantly when non-graduates leaders undermine the values of graduates' qualifications. The tendency to misplace, give unappropriated tasks, or even assign a graduate a subordinate position where he cannot apply his knowledge or skills are among the challenges. Sometimes, these practices may lead to a sour relationship between the leader and the graduate, hence failure for the graduate to apply the acquired knowledge and skills. Indeed, graduate learning can be observed by the tasks they perform, and that wrong task may provide false information and evaluation of their learning.

Indeed, I have not defined what learning is, but I theorise to allow you to describe it based on the mentioned or other supportive hypotheses. Learning is a complex phenomenon that requires broad and diverse perspectives and high investigation in defining. Besides, one must have high critical thinking and comprehend the learning goals to describe learning. Importantly, no matter how one defines it, the person should understand that it is complex due to its task and contextual dependence. Likewise, to support you in defining learning in HE, I will discuss the learning content in the next chapter. Understanding the learning content in HE may lead to the appropriate definition of learning and the prediction of the skills graduates are expected to have acquired.

However, be aware that learning level is different from the level of education because the level of education cannot guarantee individual learning. People may learn more materials than the level of education they have completed or vice versa, and that labelling people based on their education levels is not a practice to encourage. Therefore, I want to avoid evaluating peoples' understanding based on their levels of education, although I need people to respect the formal education evaluation system as an informant and the modifier of peoples' performances.

Figure five attempts to summarise the diverse theories one can develop when defining higher education learning.

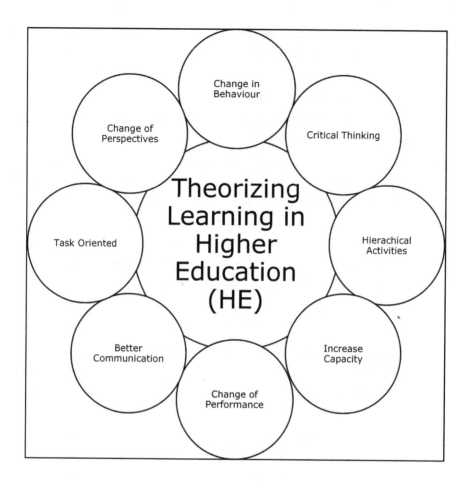

Figure 5. Learning Theories in Higher Education

Figure five informs various learning concepts one can employ to define learning. First, learning is a process of critical thinking that changes someone's perception, performance, and behaviour. Second, the process occurs hierarchically, from remembering information to creating knowledge and utilize it in problem-solving at a higher level of education. Third, learning is task-oriented and increases learners' capacity to communicate knowledge and increase performance.

Self-Reflection

What theoretical framework do scholars apply in defining learning?

To what extent do you support the behaviourists' definition of learning?

How will you benefit from HE learning?

What are the attributes expected of a learned individual?

How do you theorise learning from your own perspective?

Is there a relationship between learning and individual behaviour?

What do you desire to learn in HE?

Do you think tasks create an opportunity to express individual learning?

How do you think learning in HE will support you to express the desired behaviour?

Do you think learning in HE differs from other levels of education? Explain

What are the differences in learning between lower levels of education and that of HE?

Assume you are a supervisor; how could you maximise students' learning experience?

Chapter VI
The Major Learning Contents

There are significant areas of knowledge expected of graduates. Understanding how to position graduates for better utilisation of their skills, competencies, and knowledge is vital. The process of graduate placement in the job market might be more straightforward if the stakeholders understand what HE students learn. Although there are different universities worldwide with different faculties, departments, disciplines, and subjects, there are core learning contents that almost all successful graduates have learned before graduation. The vital topics learned regardless of structures, practices, and the learning context or the nature of the student's degree. Understanding these core learning contents may lead to appropriate assessing graduates' qualifications and assigning them proper tasks. It may also help graduates to comprehend their qualifications for them to create employment.

Most employers need to understand the areas of learning HEIs. Currently, based on my conversation with some employers, the hiring of HE graduates undergoes little information about their learning process, achievement, and capabilities. Although they anticipate graduates to have attained a certain standard of knowledge, skills, and competencies, the majority are unaware of the specific knowledge and skills that legitimises their occupation of certain positions and tasks in the job market (Crebert et al., 2004). Employers are also uncertain about the quality of graduates because of diversity in practices in most HEIs. Nevertheless, the assumption is that most graduates have some advanced knowledge rarely found in other levels of education.

Because of this ambiguity and various practices, the following section will discuss the major learning contents in HE. Almost all institutions, departments, and disciplines that award a degree worldwide focus on these main standard learning contents. Likewise, students are assessed and graded in these areas to ensure their mastering of the contents before graduation. Therefore, I will discuss these learning contents in HE randomly without ranking them.

Indeed, students in most HEIs learn some materials that are useful in societal development. Among others are:

How to Research

Learning how to research is vital content for almost all HE students. Since establishing a research degree in Germany, conducting research has been the essential aspect of the HE learning curriculum (Simpson, 1983). According to Connell & Manathunga (2012), in the 1960s, students were required to formulate a research project of their own, and they researched independently under less support from a supervisor. Most students were supervised by a supervisor who was a specialist in the field and who had the research skills. However, research learning in the traditional era was observed as weak and unsuccessful by some scholars. As I mentioned earlier, people have different opinions on the quality, but research was the most critical learning content. Similarly, scholars Clark (2007) and Kelly (2017) contended that students were expected to be competent in research and contribute critically to their discipline with original research-based knowledge.

The importance of research, learning was supported by Kelly (2005) when discussing the supervisors' conceptualisation of good research, she asserted that:

"...Well-presented, significant, important, communicated, well-written, novel ideas, scholarly, archival" and when defining a good researcher, she contended: "... Creative, good with ideas, inventive, open-minded, enthusiastic, well-read, a good communicator, persuasive, self-critical, adaptable."(p. 250).

Indeed, the mentioned are among the qualifications expected of graduates. Therefore, undertaking research involves different stages that students must follow systematically. In addition, students ought to perform multiple tasks involving communication with various learning agencies for information and guidance.

Several scholars (Kiley & Mullins (2005), Kiley & Wisker (2010), and (Wisker, Robinson, Trafford, Lilly & Warnes, 2004)) have provided in-depth procedures that students must follow when conducting research. These include a choice of a researchable problem and the source of information. Remember, not all problems can be investigated scientifically; some problems require spiritual solutions. However, students learn how to identify a problem and find information about it that can lead to strategies to finding solutions. Finding information requires students to formulate some fundamental questions to lead to thinking and collecting the required information. Therefore, students learn how to construct research questions and objectives as an effective strategy for gathering information. The choice of a research topic and the formulation of research objectives/questions (Amundsen & Wilson, 2012) are the essential elements of the research learning required of students.

Most students in HE are regarded as problem solvers and that they have particular philosophical ideologies. Their thought supports them in creating or utilising the available research paradigms and theories to bring new knowledge and solutions. Although sometimes research can reproduce theories that can be developed or verified by other studies (Creswell & Plano Clark, 2018), most of the time, students ought to place their studies within a particular theoretical framework. Therefore, students learn to research following systematic theoretical procedures that they ought to master and communicate their results. Therefore, regardless of the student's type of degree and learning practices, HE's primary learning content is research. Indeed, a researcher must follow some ethics in order for his investigation to be reliable and meaningful to the intended groups.

Ethics Procedures

Research students learn to observe academic ethics. There are many issues that one should observe, but importantly researcher ethics are the number one issue students ought to examine carefully before conducting research (Anderson & Caldwell (2017), Berg (2009)). Therefore, students learn how to perceive ethics needed when dealing with participants during the research process. Among others, they learn how to protect the participants and their privacy (Wiles, Crow, Heath, & Charles, 2008). In addition, the research context, meaning the natural environment (the area, the class, or land), should be protected and respected by the researcher, and any harm may lead to negative consequences and even legal measures.

Ethics include the sharing of the information provided. A researcher needs to inform his participants how the information will be handled and how the participants' identity will be protected where required (Taylor (2015), Toulson (2006). Sometimes the research outcomes may be shared with a third party depending on the purpose of the research. The intention and procedures of sharing information ought to be known by the participants from the very beginning. By reading the references, you will understand the procedures to follow and the importance of informing the participants of the purpose of the research. In addition, participants should comprehend how the information and the research outcomes will be shared. Some researchers' objectives involve producing new knowledge that can support problem-solving or altering a participant's life. The research objectives must be communicated clearly with the source of information, i.e., the participants.

For example, let us say a researcher is researching child abuse. He should carefully obtain permission from children's parents/guardians to involve children in data collection. The issue of permission depends on the age of the children, and the researcher must observe research ethics and the agreement with the participants. It is also vital to notify the participants of the research purpose and ensure that the information will only be used for the research purposes conveyed (Creswell, Plano Clark, Gutmann, & Hanson (2003), Creswell (2018a, 2018b), Creswell & Plano Clark (2007)).

For example, if the research purpose is to inform the stakeholders about the state of children, then the information will be shared with the intended people for this purpose. Likewise, if the research aims to solve the problem, the information will be shared with people who can solve the problem. The information might be shared with a third party for awareness or to solve the problems in these cases. Indeed, the researcher ought to communicate the research purpose to the participants in detail and clearly without hiding anything. Therefore, the purpose of research is the critical determinant of their participation and cooperation. If the intended participants disagree with the researching procedures and the preservation or sharing of information, they are free to terminate their participation. Indeed, participants may withdraw their participation anytime when they desire, and they should receive this information about their freedom at the beginning of their cooperation. Ethically, the researcher (student) is not supposed to threaten the intended participants when not participating, and their decision should not jeopardise any of their privileges.

Moreover, confidentiality and anonymity are issues to clarify. For example, the participants and the researcher should sign a contract in their cooperation that guides them of their scope and teamwork strategies. Indeed, it is not the issue of signing papers and the agreement forms, but sincerity, honesty, and care of the participants and their environment (Onwuegbuzie, Dickinson, Leech, & Zoran

(2009). Such involvement in participants' wellbeing is one way of appreciating and ensuring no danger for them, neither their loved ones nor the environment. This kind of integrity further preserves the information to not land in the hands of inappropriate people or organisations. The sensitive research information should be handled with care so that the research causes no harm.

For example, the issue of child abuse mentioned earlier, the participants may inform the research about the people they believe had conducted child abuse actions. The information is sensitive and may harm both the victims and the attackers if not well handled. It might be a risk to preserve this information in a regular computer program or files because it might be accessible in one way or the other (Toulson, 2006). Today humans face challenges caused by hackers who have no respect for a person or information. So, with sensitive information, a researcher might need to communicate with only the appropriate people (if that was the agreement) and preserve it in a particular protected data program or other nonviolent means for such sensitive information.

In addition, the research results should be trustworthy. The students are required to indicate the issue of validity and reliability of the information. The way students observe procedures required for the research with integrity, handling the information carefully and objectively, and respecting the participants' privacy are among the indicators of observing research validity. Likewise, the interpretation of the information, especially interview responses, should be conducted without purposive biases (Noble & Smith, 2015). The research students must produce reliable information such that whoever needs to repeat the same research may also verify its reliability. The consistency of the information and the observation of appropriate research methods and ethics influence the trustworthiness of the research findings.

For more information about the scope and details concerning research reliability and validity, one can read the references in this book. In addition, students might be required to perceive additional rules stipulated by the host university that are relevant and important to ensure the quality of the information and the research results in general. These are among ethics that students ought to learn, observe, and apply when conducting research. Fortunately, the ethics learned in HE apply to diverse situations in our lives if well communicated.

Learn How to Communicate

In addition, HE students learn how to communicate. There is no way a graduate can escape consultation with different learning agencies. As I discussed in the learning section, students interact with peers, academics, non-academic staff, diverse sources of information, and participants (in field research). In addition, students communicate with objects such as computers, laboratory apparatus, and facilities, gymnastic equipment, dance floors (to mention a few) during their learning, depending on their field and their interests. Communication with subjects and objects in HE is inevitable, and students must learn how to navigate their communication with other agencies at all times.

Indeed, self-communication plays a significant role in peoples' lives. All individuals, including students, communicate with themselves in different situations. For example, some students converse with themselves to check on their actions, appearances, and thinking. They might interact consciously or unconsciously, but this communication occurs and develops students in different and unique ways (Besti, 2006). Students may also find it beneficial to communicate with themselves in various decision-making situations to evaluate the consequences. Therefore, students' self-communication can help them better understand their weaknesses, strengths, and needs. In addition, the communication may help students identify the area they need to direct more effort or demand more support or other issues. Even students who decide to drop out of their studies, it is a result of self-communication. Sometimes, one may think she is isolated, abandoned, neglected, and that is part of self-communication that may lead to dropout.

Without a doubt, self-communication is vital in all areas of human life. Several issues lead me to believe that students communicate with "self" more than they do with other people. First, students would not learn if they had no communication with "self" that support them to identify a shortage of knowledge and the skills and competencies they need. I also think that self-communication goes for all aspects of decision-making in their learning and helps students understand what they need or ought to perform. For example, the students reading this book have communicated with "self" and realise that they need more information about HE and that the book can provide what they need. They have reflected on themselves and realise areas of improvement. The students' self-conversation has helped them realise their capability and fundamental aspect of their learning goals.

Likewise, students must communicate with their participants in the field when collecting information for their research projects. Indeed, adequate, and appropriate communication is needed to convey study objectives orally and in writing to the participants. The willingness of participants depends on the explanation they receive from the students concerning research purposes. On other occasions, students need to communicate their research results with stakeholders for information or for problem-solving. Indeed, students learn to communicate and need to communicate when they apply for a degree position to their graduation. A successful student should have gone through the communication process, both orally and in writing. Therefore, communication is one of the vital contents of learning in HE, and this can be learned formally or informally through sharing of information or solving problems.

Problem Solving

Students in HE learn scientific problem-solving techniques. According to Creswell (2018a, 2018b), students in HE ought to follow research procedures in solving problems. For example, the problem and the questions lead to the choice of research method (s) and its rationale. A research method collects information to solve a research problem through systematic analysis and synthesis of data collected. The tools to utilize in data collection and analysis are essential for solving problems in many ways in real life.

The process of solving problems of any kind needs investigation of the cause of the problem. All possible information related to the problem should be discussed when finding a solution. Students need to solve problems not as anybody but as experts; they need to follow scientific procedures that differentiate them from other problem solvers. For example, students who have mastered research work have a better chance of solving the problem scientifically than others. Likewise, Creswell & Plano Clark (2011), Creswell & Plano Clark (2018), Gibbs (2018) have written about procedures that need to be followed when doing research that and the kind of methods to employ. Reading the mentioned publications and others can be beneficial for students when solving problems scientifically.

The process of learning by focusing on problem-solving scientifically thorough research is vital. However, these procedures can be diverse and sometimes influenced by the context and the concepts of the problem solver. The problem-solving process accommodates diverse local and global research concepts as discussed in mixed research methods (Bergman (2008), Creswell & Plano Clark (2018), Onwuegbuzie et al. (2011)). These scholars have indicated diverse ways of solving research problems, but in mixed methods, the focus is what works best. Therefore, one can solve the problem by applying qualitative research methods, quantitative, or mixed methods research. It is not my intention to discuss each of these methods in-depth, but the references provided can be helpful for those who desire to understand more of them.

Consequently, the problem-solving process requires critical thinking, analysis, and synthesis. No matter the research method students opt for, a systematic problem-solving capability is required. Problem-solving knowledge is the most expected acquaintance and is the distinctive feature expected of HE graduates (Adams (2015), Simpson (1983)). Similarly, we must acknowledge that the scientific problem-solving ability results from sorting, comparing, and comprehending the information through critical thinking (Floyd (2011), Freire & Fraser (1997)). Likewise, Wisker et al. (2004) discussed the problem-solving ability expected of graduates, and they identified aspects of learning that support research students to solve problems. Reading their writing may be beneficial for those who need more information about meta-learning and meta-cognition or scientific problem-solving techniques. Indeed, HE students learn how to solve problems scientifically through diverse research methods following research methods procedures. However, it is not always easy to understand whether students have learned to research, solve a problem, and other learning contents without testing them. Therefore, HE students are provided with assignments to communicate their knowledge in writing to legitimate their understanding to their examiners.

Students Learn How to Write

Most HEIs empower their students by teaching them how to write. Students write several assignments, essays, project reports, term papers, and thesis during their learning. The writing can be submitted individually and collaboratively where two or more students combine their ideas in writing. For example, in most universities, writing short assignments and term papers is a part of a formative evaluation required, and the writing of the thesis or dissertation is required in the summative evaluation (Lee & Kamler (2008), McAlpine & Amundsen (2012), Palmer (2012)). Currently, students, especially in master's and doctoral degree levels, are encouraged to write scholarly articles collaboratively for publications, and this is one of the governmental and institutional policies (Aitchison & Guerin

(2014), Wisker (2015)). In writing, students argue and apply critical thinking, challenging their perspectives and the writing of others.

However, learning how to write may be a challenging practice. Most students in HE struggle with writing, and some teachers have little expertise in guiding students in writing (Carter & Kumar, 2017). I guess the challenge of writing is more vivid for students whose language of instruction/the writing language is different from their first language and even different from their previous language of instruction. My guess is confirmed by Connell and Manathunga (2012), who asserted that:

There are a lot of debates about where the boundaries are when providing feedback on students' writing for students whose first language is not English (p. 8)

Indeed, language is power and important as reliable information. For example, one cannot acquire information without mastering the language which carries the required information. As well writing requires mastering the language and reading other people's writings to convey the information.

In addition, the assessment in HE is conducted differently but requires written documents. This is to say, almost all universities worldwide are keen to assess written documents from students, and they are encouraged to publish while studying. The current system of publication has led learning to write to be even more critical. Writing skills are essential during HE learning and beyond; that is the primary reason supervisors must enhance and assist students to acquire qualifications. Unfortunately, most supervisors assume students have acquired writing skills before joining HE, and the assumption hinders them from providing adequate support (Carter & Kumar, 2017). Some universities apply different methods apart from supervisors' assistance to ensure that students learn to write appropriately. There are diverse programmes to assist students with their writing, such as workshops, seminars, and even blogs (Byrne (1979), Guerin, Carter, & Aitchison (2015), Lee & Kamler (2008), Wolff (2010)).

Learning how to write is even facilitated by the diverse ways of obtaining a degree. There is a possibility of acquiring master's and doctoral degrees by the publication today Lee & Kamler, 2008). The well-written publications are preferred, and most universities have increased the importance of learning how to write (Carter (2011), Lee & Kamler (2008), O'Collins (2011)). Writing competencies are required by many organisations, especially academic institutions and organisations that work with information dissemination. One of the employers I met at the conference I described earlier informed me about his organisation and the need for qualified writers. His explanation made me realise that writing skills are vital not only in an academic environment but in non-academic organisations. Thus, students in HE learn how to write, and their skills can be applied to several writing activities that require writing reports, project proposals, policies, and other information.

Please note: It might be difficult for someone to be a good writer if he is not a good reader, thinker, and analyser. Thus, writing skills go hand in hand with other skills such as intercultural skills, language skills, digital skills, presentation skills, and even teaching skills that I cannot discuss in this book. I should admit that it is a challenge to mention all that HE students learn, but the already mentioned areas of learning can provide an insight to those who desired to study in HE to understand the core areas of learning. In addition, the information can support them in their evaluation of whether they are ready to learn the contents. For example, if a person thinks he has adequate recognisable knowledge of the areas I mentioned, he may need to update his knowledge and fill the gaps in the already acquired knowledge.

No doubt, the mentioned learning contents can be acquired in other levels of education too. So, if you have read my explanation and understand that I ignore the learning acquired from other levels of education, you did not get my message appropriately. People can be good writers, communicators and researchers without HE. However, because my topic is to inform people about HE practices and support them with information to make a decision, I am not obliged to promote or disvalue other levels of education, and that is why I must focus on HE and display what is happening there.

Undoubtedly, there is much useful knowledge acquired through other levels of education that may be discussed in other writings. The way this writing favors HE and graduates is not something to apologise for but is a purposive way intended to inform people who desire to learn or update their information about HE. So to say, HEIs produce people who have learned, among other things, to research and to communicate appropriately with wide subjects and objects. In addition, the individuals learn fundamental ethics and communication, both in writing and orally, to convey information or solve problems. These five major topics discussed in this section are among many of the contents HE students learn.

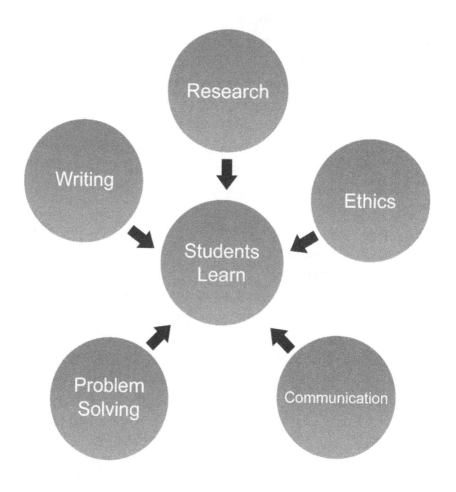

Figure 6. Five Main Learning Content in Higher Education

Higher education students learn several issues, but they cannot avoid learning the topics indicated in figure six. All higher education students learn researching, writing, and problem-solving strategies. Moreover, students must learn how to communicate with others, including with supervisors and other learning agencies. They also must abide by academic and non-academic ethics in their learning, especially researching.

Self-Reflection

What contents do you desire to learn in HE?

Do you understand ethics related to the use of literature?

How do you think teachers can prevent plagiarism in HE?

Do you think learning must be related to problem-solving?

What is your desire? To learn individually or with other students?

To what extent do you think governmental policies dominate in HE?

How can students be involved in planning learning content?

Is it that research is important in HE learning? Explain

What are the procedures that one should follow when doing research?

What is your research topic? And what is your area of study?

Do you think HE learning content should be locally organized or globally?

Is there a relationship between success in learning and problem-solving ability?

Chapter VII
How do Students Learn

Currently, most universities have two types of learning contexts. The physical and the digital learning, and there is no clear cut between these two learning contexts. Some physical learning can lead to digital learning and vice versa, and there is no limit of content or discipline to learn in these two contexts. For example, students in, let's say, philosophy class where a discussion about project management is being conducted may decide to examine the scholarly literature and the research conducted in this area online. Students can also opt for lectures online for supplements of what was learned in a physical context. The class conducted in a physical context can end up with the scholarly literature examined online. It has been a norm to include a digital search for more information on the issues discussed in physical learning. Likewise, students may have online courses, but they might need more information, leading to contact with teachers in a physical context. Physical learning and digital learning are applied interchangeably in HE today. However, I will discuss these two kinds of learning contexts briefly and separately.

The Physical Learning Context

Traditionally, it was costly to access HE learning. Besides, the learning was in the university premises and not from a distance. Students had to attend a physical university campus, and there were no other means of learning than to meet substantially in the learning context. In addition, physical learning was costly, as Simpson (1983) described, he informed the cost associated with HE in Germany, and students from other parts of Europe and the United States had to reside in Germany. Pointing out the doctorate degrees, Simpson added that the cost was high, and this was among the catalysts that forced the United States to establish its doctoral degree to minimise the cost of sending young men abroad

(Germany). This explanation indicates that students could access learning if they attend in a physical learning environment.

However, apart from the cost of the physical learning style, there were numerous advantages of learning in a physical environment. Indeed, learning in a physical environment has been popular for centuries, although current technology facilitates online learning. Some of the benefits of physical learning still exist today, and one is that students learn from the teachers and the institution's natural settings. Indeed, teachers and institutions have a message to students, meaning that the natural setting of HEIs provides students with information that cannot be obtained and learned otherwise. For example, the learning environment has several values, norms, and cultures that need to be learned, including the language and people's communication styles. Sometimes, unwritten values and norms can be observed by students for them to cope with the learning environment and its agencies.

Furthermore, it is advantageous for students to interact with physical learning contexts and people when researching and beyond (Manathunga, 2009). For example, if a student is enrolled in one of the universities, let us say, in Tanzania or Norway, where the language of instruction may be different from that of indigenous people and everyday language of interaction. In this case, students can be motivated to learn the Swahili language of Tanzania to communicate with people outside the university. In the case of Norway, the students may learn the Norwegian language to simplify understanding of what is going on in society.

Therefore, in these two cases, the institutions or donors and languages will learn the subjects intended for them. In addition, learning the language in natural physical settings may support the students in learning the university's community's unwritten cultural values and norms. It might be difficult for this kind of cultural learning to happen outside this natural setting. Thus, learning in a physical environment facilitates the acquisition of diverse knowledge associated with the institution and the institution's community.

Likewise, learners learn from peers with whom they interact in the physical learning context. Peer contributions are essential in modifying the values and culture of each other and sometimes can lead to an inclusive learning community. The interactions with other learning agencies in the physical environment may also result in cooperation in finding solutions to some academic and even social challenges that individual students may have faced. For example, students may have a computer problem that another student on the premises can solve.

131

Likewise, the student, who solved the computer problem, can be grateful for the arena to share his knowledge with others. So, this sharing of knowledge is vital for students and possible in the physical learning environment.

In many cases, students have some knowledge that is required of others and hence mutual sharing is beneficial. As Boud and Lee (2005) explained in their article about peer learning, students learn through, from, and with peers. Indeed, students' association helps them learn and adjust to each other's values and modify their beliefs, practices, and behavior in general. Thus, students in a physical setting normally connect with themselves and various learning agencies that rarely exist in other settings.

According to Boud and Lee (2005), there are several advantages associated with peer learning. First, students tend to learn how to communicate through feedback from each other, and that the provision and reception of feedback need some knowledge and understanding of each other's interests. Therefore, students need to interact with others to comprehend their perceptions and enhance positive cooperation among students. Second, students' ability to receive and provide feedback to peers may eventually support them to prepare and understand the supervisors' advice better. Likewise, the experiences students acquire from peers in their interactions support them in communicating their weaknesses and strengths openly. Hence, when they cooperate and practice their communication appropriately, they succeed in their learning. Third, peer learning develops a team spirit vital for students in their collaboration with learning agencies and beyond. Thus, to understand the importance of peer learning, one may consult Boud and Lee's (2005) article and others discussing this topic.

Generally, physical learning provides instant feedback vital in learning. The feedback can be of various forms, such as through the body language of the participants. When interacting with people physically, one can observe their body reactions and translate the message. In other kinds of learning, students and the teachers can hide their body reactions to a certain extent, but in physical learning, where they meet and see each other, their feelings can be observed through their body reactions instantly. Reading the body of a learner or a teacher can provide vital information and even correct or adjust one's mind without further discussion (Morgan, Eliot, Lowe, & Gorman, 2016). Therefore, it is essential to care for other people's feelings and non-verbal reactions in learning, which is provided mainly through the physical environment.

Physical learning can occur in different ways. In the following section, I will briefly discuss how students may learn in a physical learning environment. Then, I will focus on three major components of physical context: observation, acculturation, and data collection.

Through Observation

Students learn in a physical context informally and formally through observation. As I pointed out earlier, learning with others in a classroom does not limit students to learn only the intended contents, but also other unintended issues such as each other's culture, beliefs, and behaviour. It is problematic for HE teachers to teach students everything they need to know. Exposing students to the physical setting in an academic environment where they tend to learn what they desire can be beneficial. Students can observe the activities and the actors in the learning environment by themselves, and this has been part of the teaching strategy applied in most HE (Goldthorpe, 2007).

For example, the students who happened to join their supervisors/teachers in academic workshops, seminars, or any other gatherings, learn unwritten protocols and principles by observation. These gatherings (seminars, workshops, meetings, and experiments) are essential where students interact with other learning agencies, apart from their teachers. The process unfolds some information that supports students with diverse knowledge and skills needed in their careers. They may learn how people communicate, who does what in an academic context, the politics surrounding HEIs, and the general community. There is evidence that students learn informally and formally through observation and participation in different occasions (Eraut, 2004). It is also believed that this kind of learning effectively moulding students' behaviour and skills acquisition.

Learning through observation is acknowledged by scholars. For example, Grant (2005, 2008) asserted that students learn informally from their supervisors' attributes in supervision. She proclaimed that supervisors should observe their behavior because students pick what they see from them and practice later in their teaching. Likewise, Lee (2007)) accredited; most supervisors supervise students the way they were self-supervised, and her statement indicates learning by observation. Indeed, although some university teachers do not teach students some issues, students learn by observing their practices. The case of students learning from their supervisors without formal courses is evidence of learning by observation even though learning is not limited to a specific method.

Acculturation Process

In other cases, physical learning occurs through acculturation in HE. In this process, students apply their values, norms, and culture into the learning environment and modify them accordingly. Amundsen & McAlpine (2009), Chiappetta-Swanson (2011), Lee (2008) discussed how students learn the culture of their fields, the department, and the discipline through exposure. Students are exposed to academics and scholarly communities to learn the cultures and protocols related to the academic communities while modifying their own culture and learning environment (Bourdieu, 2013). It is not the intention of this writing to discuss acculturation intensely, but if you need to widen your knowledge about it, you may need to read an article by Berry (2003) and others. Again, seminars, workshops, and other academic gatherings can also be good arenas for acculturation.

Some people have difficulty separating acculturation and enculturation. Enculturation is a lifelong process where all individuals acquire certain cultures of their environment, family, clan, community, and even race and nation. Several aspects indicate individual cultures, such as clothing, food, beliefs, arts, and other traditions that differentiate the person from other people from other communities. The main facilitators for this first individual socialisation are family members, parents/guardians and relatives, peers, and even co-workers (Bourdieu, 2013). These agencies ensure that the new member of the family or community, or country has acquired social skills that are distinctive and significant for his identity and belonging to the group.

As I mentioned earlier, HEIs have a policy of increasing international students with diverse cultural backgrounds. The students ought to conform to the institution and academic culture through acculturation, the mix of cultures. The process can happen through informal or formal learning depending on how the individuals encounter these secondary socialization agencies. For example, students in HE contact different learning agencies with different cultures beyond the academic culture, especially during the research activities in data collection (Manathunga, 2009). Therefore, these cultures meet with the individual student's own culture, and the intermingling leads to acculturation.

For example, a supervisor informed me that most research students from developing countries, who obtain the opportunity to study in western countries, usually opt to conduct research projects in their countries of origin because they are more familiar with people who can provide them with the information they need. As a result, most students transfer or share the culture they have acquired in the learning environment abroad during this data collection process. Some of these cultures can be a language where they speak a foreign language more often than before, dress differently from others of their home countries and even cook or eat different food from the majority. Thus, the management of primary and secondary, whether occurring unconsciously or consciously, is part of acculturation.

In other cases, a student may take responsibility as a research assistant while working with experienced researchers. In this way, he will interact with some cultures that were not known to him. Some students may be required to work on their research but consult the experienced researchers for information through questionnaires or interviews as participants or advisors (Berry, 2003). Others have undergone acculturation by being exposed to other cultures and integrating their own culture into the new environment. These processes can result in an amalgamation of students' culture and the secondary cultures from their learning environment. The more flexible the students are in conceptualizing their own culture concerning others, the easier the acculturation. However, if a student thinks that his culture is the best of all and fail to integrate with other cultures, he may graduate without learning.

Likewise, McAlpine, Amundsen, and Sarikaya (2017) demonstrated that the socialisation of students in a physical learning context is vital for students to learn from each other and integrate their cultures. Likewise, Devos, Boudrenghien, Van der Linden, Azzi, Frenay, Galand, Klein (2017) reminded us that the socialisation of students might be an inspiration for students to work effectively and a measure for hindering attrition. Sometimes, students require extrinsic motivation and a helping hand to integrate with two or more cultures, and that is why Wisker (2005) proposed the strategies that supervisors can apply to support students in the process of acculturation. She mentioned two techniques the supervisors may employ, thus, encouraging students to attend relevant conferences and seminars and motivating students to produce collaborative publications. Again, in most cases, the student's initiative in associating with multicultural and multidisciplinary learning environments can result in sustainable acculturation (Manathunga (2017), Manathunga et al. (2017), Morgan et al. (2016)).

Through Data Collection

Normally, students' contact with participants in a physical learning arena can facilitate their learning. Participants, who are the sources of scientific information for students' projects, modify students' thoughts and belief patterns. Through communication, sometimes face-to-face interviews with participants or telephone and other means (Morgan et al., 2016). Indeed, students obtain an insight into how the actual physical world of academics operates when gathering information. They learn where scientific information comes from, how to handle the data obtained objectively, and the consequences of information biases (Bergman (2008), Creswell et al. (2003)). In addition, students may interact with significant people and key players in the field and (informant and supervisors) those who can influence their project. Such experience creates a sense of responsibility and a high level of academic maturation, as discussed in the ethics session earlier. Without a doubt, students learn some procedures to follow when conducting data collection as described by many scholars, including (Creswell et al. (1994, 2003, 2005, 2015, 2018), Gibbs (2018)), to mention a few. Therefore, understanding the procedures for data collection and its application may support students in learning academic environment practices. The understandings may also support them in the modification of their values, norms, and cultures.

Moreover, the data collection process teaches students to be responsible. For example, students are accountable for caring physically, mentally, and emotionally for the participants' safety. They are also responsible for all other aspects of participants' wellbeing for the whole period they are dealing with the project. Students are allowed to be shaped by the participants' thoughts and behavior patterns on the research topic. Students learn to be a good listeners while participants usually play the active role and are essential agencies to challenge and stretch the students' understanding of the issue they are dealing with (Manathunga, 2009). Hence, students' and informants' experiences and feedback modify their thoughts and beliefs about the research problem by creating new knowledge.

Indeed, physical learning style is beneficial not only for students but all involved. Some research participants in a physical context obtain an opportunity to reflect on their situations concerning the research problem and questions scientifically. The interview questions are conducted in a natural setting (Fusch & Ness, 2015; Onwuegbuzie et al., 2009), where participants and researchers have an opportunity to extend their conversation. Such conversational interviews tend to capture information that could not be obtained in another context than physical and face-to-face. For example, a researcher can support the participants to reflect on the issues more deeply. Even if there is a serious problem, sometimes, a solution can be found through this kind of extended conversation. Therefore, data collection creates a useful learning and sharing arena between the researchers and the participants. Furthermore, the interaction may modify the participants' values, norms, culture, and research students.

However, not all learning in HE is conducted in a physical environment these days. In this case, students have not always had an opportunity to learn by observing their learning environment neither learning agencies. Likewise, in some cases in HE learning, students are not required to learn secondary culture due to interaction limitations. Besides, the majority is not engaged in data collection that requires conversational interviews with participants in their physical settings. Currently, most students prefer learning through digital medium, and even data collection can be through diverse digital programmess. Therefore, it might be useful to discuss digital learning, meaning the online environment. First, however, to remind ourselves, we have three major physical learning conditions, as shown in figure seven.

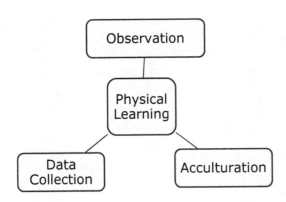

Figure 7. Three Major Medium of Physical Learning

Figure seven shows that students in HE can learn through observation when exposed to the learning environment. In addition, they can learn through data collection in natural settings while communicating with the environment and participants. Further, they may learn through acculturation by exchanging their norms, values, and cultures with others. These are a few of the many ways HE students learn.

Self-Reflection

What do you think can be done better for HE students' physical learning?

Do you think physical learning must be enhanced in the current digital learning era?

What are some disadvantages of physical learning?

What do you think students benefits from physical learning?

Do you think supervisors must be responsible for creating students' conducive physical learning environment?

What problem do students encounter in a physical learning context?

Do you think students require some skills to learning in a physical environment?

Do you think students researching by literature review can acquire skills learned in a physical learning environment?

How do you theorise a physical learning environment?

What are the advantages and disadvantages of acculturation?

What do you think can support students in learning better through observation?

Would you advise how HEIs can organise physical learning to benefit their students?

Chapter VIII
The Digital Learning Context

The digital learning environment in HE can cater to multiple purposes. Currently, the HE learning context has been dominated by digital appliances. This revolution in learning results from the advancement of technology and the accessibility of internet (Lillejord, Børte, Nesje, & Ruud, 2018). Most universities have diverse digital learning programmes that students may access on their self-learning and with learning agencies. Sometimes they obtain guidance from their learning agencies where both physical and digital learning is applied. The students ought to master computer, most of the times different computer programmes to access some learning programmes. Therefore, students must acquire computer skills to benefit from digital programmes and search relevant information from different databases (Bowen, 2013).

For example, students may have access to different publications online. They are required to have mastered some different searching database programmes to access the information. Other publications need special codes provided to students by the institution and require students to follow some procedures when accessing online learning materials. For example, let us say students need to access a publication by Wisker, *"The Good Supervisor"* (2005, 2012), they first need to master computer and the database that allow the reading of the documents. I believe the first area online where most students start their searching is Google Scholar. In this database, there are some publications that everybody can access, and others may have special programmes that protect and control access. Normally, students have access to the learning institution to have extended access and a wide range of literature.

Students need access to read some of the online publications. Individual student needs to find out the scope of his access and the specific databases that are accessible. Some countries and universities allow private people who are not enrolled in their institutions to access the scholarly information upon particular agreement (you may need to find out). For example, if you are a student, check your accessibility of scholarly information, and if you think you should have more access, you must contact the responsible people to provide you with the access you need. You may also find out the procedures to follow to be a member of other libraries that are not affiliated with the learning institution to widen the range of information sources.

This kind of online learning in HE has been discussed by several scholars (Bowen (2013), Lever-Duffy (2008), Price & Rogers (2004), Xu, Shevchenko, Lavery, Semrau, Liga, Alvarado, Bayvel (2017)). The scholars maintained that the diversity in HE has resulted in the formulation of learning support units with digital workshop programmes open for students in many universities. Most supporting units require students to have some qualities such as self-evaluation, self-discipline, and self-management to benefit from the programs. Students can access the learning contents at any time, and, in some cases, students may decide what to learn by selecting the available programs. Thus, university students require no permission to engage in digital learning, which is why self-management and control are vital.

Self-discipline is vital in a digital learning environment. Besides, one should have intrinsic motivation, and that acquiring knowledge must become a driving force; otherwise, it may be a disadvantage. The challenge is that teachers and other learning agencies become less involved in learning because anyone can deliver the content. Therefore, teachers are not solely the owners or sources of information to the students online. If you refer to the traditional era of HE, you can remember that teachers were like dictionaries to their students and the sole sources of information. Currently, the students are provided with the freedom and flexibility to choose sources of learning materials and access world literature.

However, online learning may disadvantage undisciplined students because they might wander around diverse information, wasting valuable time. Furthermore, students who are not disciplined may be disadvantaged by wandering around the information combined with unlimited social media that might be destructive. In addition, the wide access to learning materials needs students' intrinsic self-management capabilities. Unfortunately, there is minimal guidance to students on utilizing online information effectively in their learning. Therefore, it requires discipline to learn online, and students should be capable of dealing with unlimited social media that might be destructive and deprive their time. So, broad access to learning materials is not always advantageous if the user is not focused, structured, and has intrinsic motivation and self-management.

As mentioned earlier, students can access worldwide information online, which may require knowledge on how to apply technology and limit the scope appropriately (Bowen (2013). Indeed, most students need guidance to learn through technology and find the relevant digital content or information, especially at the beginning of their learning. Although many people think digital learning is a straightforward and quick learning approach, it is not always that way. Undeniably it provides more independence and freedom than physical, depending on learners' ability to navigate and utilise the technology purposively. Nevertheless, it does require much pre-preparation, like in the physical learning context. For example, one should be clear of the topic and significantly limit the searching to the specific pertinent area of interest. Some universities assist students through seminars and workshops on how to search literature from different databases and deal with reviews literature. Therefore, people who desire to join HE should prepare for digital learning and acquire some self-discipline before commencing. If one has a habit of jumping from one source of information to another, such as from Google to YouTube to Facebook, E-mails, Twitter, and others, he will waste time learning online.

There is a possibility of obtaining diverse support when learning through technology. The multiple assistance can happen through meetings, workshops, seminars, or even quick online chatting. For seminars and workshops, the students ought to register in some universities, and, in some cases, one needs guidance, and teaching may obtain it individually or in a group. In addition, there is a considerable possibility to combine digital learning with physical learning, especially when the students need assistance within the university campus. For example, a student might desire to learn courses online, let us say, in referencing but is uncertain how to select the appropriate referencing programmes and apply it to his writing. Sometimes, not all the information about the referencing programmes is provided, and understandable online. In such cases, tutoring is required to elaborate online information in a physical setting, and that physical learning may be combined with digital.

Let us say students are required to learn referencing programs such as RefWorks, Zotero, EndNote, and Mendeley (to name a few). Although these programs have tutorials online, some students may need a lecturer or a physical tutorial to ask questions and obtain other support in a physical environment.

Sometimes, students may benefit from examples that elaborate on some issues when combining physical interactions. Other times, the students may lack access to all the information required to understand the programmes at hand online. In such cases, the students might also need to attend a workshop to receive more guidance or access links to support them. Therefore, it might be beneficial for the students to attend the physical setting where they contact learning agencies to assist them with extended questions.

Similarly, digital learning applies to students' evaluations. Most supervisors' feedback on students' writing is mainly provided electronically, where students read the comments and discuss their work with their supervisors. For example, students' written work may be exchanged and evaluated by a supervisor or more using a different coloured programme differentiating their work from that of the students electronically. Students can also respond to the feedback from the supervisor(s), and the writing can be exchanged back and forth electronically by both parties until they are satisfied. Digital communication in evaluation is vital because students and teachers can observe their development from the beginning of their cooperation to the final stage. It might be a good way for students to reflect on their progress and understand what it takes to acquire the writing skills required in HE.

Likewise, digital academic communication is essential. Students and learning agencies can interconnect through Facebook, Twitter, Google Docs, blogs (Guerin et al., 2015), and other online web pages and programmes. Indeed, students can participate in valuable discussions and acquire knowledge. In addition, some supervisors have web pages where they inform students and other users of updated issues and topics in their field. For instance, students can access information about the projects the supervisors are interested in, the various deadlines for their assignments, and researchers that are going on in their departments or institutions. Moreover, students may comprehend the upcoming seminars, workshops, academic meetings, and even social events. Indeed, digital communication has become a vital arena for academics to interconnect with themselves and the world.

However, digital learning might be complicated if students lack guidance. Most universities have changed some programs from physical settings to digital, especially with the coronavirus outbreak. Therefore, online learning is a kind of learning that has changed the education system and the way people communicate worldwide (Bowen (2013), Xu et al. (2017)). In addition, some universities provide degrees online, and students graduate without physical contact with the learning agencies, university physical context, and the courses or learning provider. Students can enroll in a university webpage and choose the courses he desires and when he desires to commence the studies if one possesses the required entry qualifications. The students are generally provided with a username and password to access the institution's digital learning content. For example, some universities in the US are known for online learning, and they accommodate students from all corners worldwide. However, the universities arrange lecturers, seminars, and workshops online where students converse with their learning agencies, and even supervision occurs through technological devices. I do not want to speak for them, but one needs to contact the universities or read their web pages for more information. Indeed, several universities provide degrees online, and their students become competent and knowledgeable like those learning in physical settings. One needs to search and contact them where possible.

No doubt, the technological learning issue has raised many conversations. The scholars, Lillejord, Børte, Nesje, and Ruud (2018) have discussed technological application in learning intensively. They also explained different learning contexts where they mentioned hybrid learning contexts and pedagogical consequences of digital learning. The kind of explanation provided by these scholars can be an added information in understanding how HE learning is digitalised for better individual preparation. Indeed, digital learning has taken the world of HE by storm, and the need for physical contact is also increasing. So, in many cases, learning in higher education is a combination of physical and digital learning.

Two Kinds of Learning Styles

Again, learning in a physical context or digital may occur individually or in a group. For example, students who enroll in online degrees tend to learn sometimes individually, although they may have group seminars online. It has become an individual decision to participate in some seminars, and it does not affect other learners' learning or grades. Contrarily, online learning can happen in groups where students are ought to attend a lecture of a sort, a workshop, or a group discussion associated with assignments. The learning might be organised so that students and their learning agencies meet online and participate in a topic as if they are in a physical classroom. They can see each other through video learning programs and hear from each other's context and contents.

According to the digital and physical learning literature, there is no clear demarcation between these two learning contexts today. However, it does not mean that there is no scholarly information that has attempted to mention the differences, but I have not gathered such information for this book. So, you may search for information about the differences and perform online searching exercises before deciding the learning context you prefer. As discussed in these chapters, online and physical learning is essential, and I do not think it is appropriate to rank them. One thing for sure is that we need more research about how to benefit from online learning and acquire the discipline required. Therefore, it is vital for those who desire to choose whether to join online learning or physical learning to conduct research that can support their decision. Nevertheless, both learning contexts (physical and digital) allow individual or group learning styles.

Individual Learning

Students learn to focus on their own learning needs individually. They are encouraged to prioritise matters vital to them while observing what is required by the institute and learning agencies. The most important issue to understand is that students' needs are the motive of all learning, whether physical or digital. For example, a student enrolled in a degree and a specific course/subject, it is because he needs it. Otherwise, he would not enrol. Choosing enrolment is a personal decision that starts from the beginning of the learning journey. After this individual decision, of course, and discipline, the student needs to observe what the education provider requires. The requirements might be reading specific rules, procedures, references, and even consulting specific people or literature in the field. The institution and the department may demand that the students' writing follow a specific format and submitting the academic work at a particular time. These are among the requirements that students should observe individually so, it all starts with individual learning.

Apart from individual preferences, external factors contribute to learning. Often, the institution or department provides instructions to an individual student by considering the institution's norms and values (Marek & Peter (2012), Stensaker et al. (2008)). Sometimes these values may not favor the students' learning, especially in this era of the knowledge economy, business-like learning, where institutions desire to maximise profits. In following the instructions, the students tend to consult other learning agencies for their assistance, views, experiences, and sometimes for their assessments. Therefore, it may be essential for each student to remind himself of, his personal needs while fulfilling the requirements in learning and considering advice from learning agencies. However, the observation of conditionalities, learning instructions, and decisions focusing on the individual expectations.

For example, students in HE should write and produce some publications. In most cases, students submit short written assignments, essays, and term papers individually. In addition, they must submit theses following a particular format of writing and referencing; the instruction is vital and should be observed individually. For example, the writing content is also expected to reflect on personal understanding of the subject or a topic. The experienced examiners can comprehend whether the individual student wrote the paper by himself or not by reading his concepts.

Finding out students' ownership of the information they deliver for assessment is vital. I asked some experienced university teachers about the validity of students' writing and how they normally guarantee the possession of the individual work, especially in this era of technology that facilitates plagiarism. They admitted that it is a challenge to identify individual work today than before the technology. Technology has facilitated strategies to plagiarize, and that is why students in most universities must take integrity courses to learn how to respect other people's properties. Moreover, examiners are supported by diverse coaching programmes that provide information about the examination and how to be a good examiner (Golding, Sharmini, & Lazarovitch (2014), Sheehan (1994), Wisker & Robinson (2014)).

Surprisingly, most of the academics I consulted ensured me that they could relate to a student and his work effortlessly, first, by examining the daily wording of the student and the style of wording provided in his writing. One of the examiners, Tomas, informed: *"Students' writing has some standard and language pattern required at each level of HE (bachelor, master and doctoral) degree. Therefore, the students' writing work can be related impeccably to the student's level of education and understanding of the issues at hand. The comparison of students daily learning progression and work produced is a technique that most academics can apply to evaluate the legitimacy of students' work. This process may be even easier for examiners, especially for those who* have had academic interaction with the students from before". Another supervisor, Antony, added: *"The standard of writing is vital to observe when finding the reliability of students' work. Whenever the student writes above or below his standard, it raises suspension, leading to the extensive scrutiny of his work. This kind of recognising the standard required of the students through the wording, writing style, and the level of students' academic ability is normally applied. This can identify the part of a paper that has been plagiarised in one way or the other. Of course, the other technique we apply is digital devices and programs to identify plagiarism and other academic dishonesties".*

These supervisors have had examiners' tasks for more than ten years. They also indicated that oral examination is another method of identifying students' honesty in academics. Students may be invited to discuss their writings to examine their understanding of the contents. Although all HE learning institutions do not conduct this procedure of oral presentation, it is an essential tool for discovering academic dishonesty. Some academics who have discussed oral examinations (Kelly, 2010) indicated the purpose of such an examination is to find out students' understanding of the topic. Indeed, the oral examination can support examiners to recognise the individual student's ownership of his work. Another supervisor, Jacob, asserted: *"The way a student defends what he/she wrote is different from defending the writing of somebody else. Likewise, the kind of questions asked by examiners ensures no loophole for deceitful. Examiners tend to ask the most fundamental questions that can detect whether the student did the work or not".*

Therefore, different measures are applied to ensure individual learning achievement. My informant, Jacob, added: *"In case of the doubt after oral examination, the student may be provided with another or other assignments under close supervision to re-examine his capability. Sometimes, with adequate evidence indicating that a student has plagiarised, the student may be disqualified".* Therefore, academics who have examiners' responsibilities ensure that students' assessment indicates individual learning achievement and the development of individual academic skills required.

I must emphasise that individual honesty is highly required in academics. Undoubtedly, genuineness is vital attribute to observe due to the importance of reliable and trustworthy examinations' results and academic works. Thus, academic results separate qualified from unqualified candidates and successful from unsuccessful so, it should be accurate. Although examiners/teachers have diverse ways of detecting dishonest acts, we must bear in mind that they are humans who are not error-free beings. So, I encourage you to be honest and demonstrate academic integrity with an intrinsic desire to enhance people's trust in the formal education results. But, again, this is an individual decision, you should observe.

Advantages of Individual Learning

Individual learning has several advantages for students. First, it is flexible, and that a student can decide when to deal with the work or when to solve the academic task without affecting other people. Freedom in learning is important, considering that students are different and have different daily schedules, needs, and life phases. For instance, the learners, whom I consulted, demonstrated different concentrations, and understanding of the learning materials in a day. Some informed that they could concentrate better in the morning hours than afternoon or evening. Others were more active in the afternoon or evening time than morning time. Few demonstrated to be nocturnal, meaning they are more active mentally at night than in the daytime. Therefore, individual learning makes it easy for these variations in concentration to be convenient to students and a choice to be made accordingly.

Another advantage of individual learning pointed out was a choice of a place of learning. A quick decision can be made when it is individual learning than a group. An individual decision does not need a discussion but is "realising a comfortable place and being seated." Normally, the place of study chosen individually tends to fit the person's needs, interests, and tasks and can increase motivation in learning. For example, when I was pursuing for a master's degree, I preferred to sit at one of the corners in a coffee bar near the university library in my learning context. I would not say I liked the silent environment that existed in the library, rather the noisy and busy environment. I could be in my impulse of studying within different waves of other peoples' vibrations and noisy around me, and I was pleased. If the coffee bar was occupied, I had to use one of the university auditorium rooms for study and with some music or even a radio beside me if no one else was around. It was possible and convenient for me, although my learning environment may be destructive for some people. Yes, I was doing me.

Individual learning has several benefits, but there are some pitfalls. For example, it could be hard to choose the learning place if I worked with other students in a group. My preference could have had some critics and could maybe cause a long discussion. However, because I was alone, I needed no one to acknowledge my choice. So, individual learning has several advantages that depend on the students' focus and personal preferences. I believe you are aware of the disadvantages of individual learning because you have had such learning. No one has not experienced individual learning in his life, whether formal or informal.

For this reason, this book will not discuss the disadvantages of individual learning. So, please write down some of the disadvantages you have encountered in your learning on the topic. While I discussed some advantages of individual learning, I think you may remember the opposite is disadvantaged, and you might have experienced them in your learning.

Group work is an alternative to individual learning. Even though learning individually in HE can be flexible and provides students with independent learning choices; currently, most students prefer to work in a group. Besides, most universities encourage students to cooperate and be inclusive in their learning. Therefore, students' cooperation in learning may be unavoidable and may bring different experiences from individual learning.

Collaborative Learning

Collaborative learning can occur in a physical or digital learning environment. Indeed, cooperation in learning can be complex, although most HEIs favour it and attempt to create such an environment for students. The style needs students to work together in two or more while solving diverse educational tasks or discussing and writing. This kind of learning consists of protocols for the member to observe for them to become productive. For example, a group should have a leader, who leads the learning, and sometimes, can make decisions on behalf of other members when necessary or by inviting members' opinions for collaborative decisions.

When I was a student in HE, the group leadership role rotated within the group so that everyone could exercise leadership responsibilities. The group's alternation of responsibilities effectively allowed members to acquire different skills, and most groups were keen on this principle. Unfortunately, I could not get someone to provide me with current group work practices in universities. You may need to find more information about group work and collaborative learning in your learning context because, without a doubt, you will be required to work in a group. So, having adequate information on how the group learning functions in your department or course might be an added advantage when working with others. First, however, let us consider some advantages and disadvantages of cooperative learning in the continuing sections.

Advantages of Cooperation

There are some advantages that students find in group work. Collaborative learning provides diverse contributions from the members that cannot be obtained from a single person. Sometimes the arguments provided in a group become an eye-opener for some members. For example, some students can describe some actions that happened to them or occurred to other abusive people. Such description may lead to conscientising others to be aware of the actions that are regarded as abusive. Contrarily, some students in the group may think otherwise depending on their cultural background and values. These are some of the tensions that may occur during a discussion, especially on sensitive cultural values and personal experiences. However, if the participants' differences are considered positively with a flexible integrated mind-set aiming to acquire diverse knowledge, the group work becomes beneficial. The opposite may lead to disagreements and even conflicts and hence unproductive.

Similarly, different assessment styles can affect group participation. However, in some cases, students are assigned group work where they may be assessed individually based on their contributions. The individual grades are possible by dividing the task amongst each group member and present a part of the assignment. The assessment in such individual grading within a group is popular today, and assessment is through individual presentations. The work can be discussed and completed in a group, where students receive feedback from group members and adjust their responses accordingly, but individuals present the assignment and are assessed and graded individually. This kind of collaborative work and individual assessment allows the students to benefit from the group members' viewpoints about the topic, evaluate their contributions, and present independently.

Most students, whom I consulted, informed me that individual assessment in a group is their preference. They think that this kind of learning forces even sluggish students to find answers to the parts of their assignment. In doing that, they tend to interact with others and contribute to their fellows' part of the assignment even though each receives different grades. Students claimed that this kind of collaboration in a group is better than when only a few individuals may contribute to finding solutions to the assignment and that all members receive the same grades.

Generally, collaborative learning, whether physical or digital, tends to facilitate many skills. For example, students acquire generic skills when working collectively, such as interpersonal skills, which are highly required in today's job market. In most cases, several national and global challenges must be solved collaboratively. Therefore, students learn to communicate with others with different ideas and backgrounds (Sluijsmans, Dochy, & Moerkerke, 1998). Apart from communication and collaboration skills development, group work supports students to be observant of rules and regulations required when working with others. In addition, collaborative learning enhanced several skills that cannot be acquired when one is working alone.

Moreover, group learning is a teacher for respecting one another's viewpoint. Working with others in a group supports students with knowledge and skills of accepting others' viewpoints, even when contradicting their thoughts. Some students may have contributions that seem strange to others, but respect must be the key to their cooperation. Let us go back to the issue of the venue where students need to meet for group work. Even though the choice may not be suitable for some students, still the rest must respect the democratic choice. Sometimes, a group of five students three may prefer a similar venue, and two may prefer another, but the preference of the three will be valid. Therefore, students who can observe simple decisions made by others may function better in the job market where cooperation is highly required.

In addition, collaborative learning can create a meeting zone for diverse cultures. The integration of cultures is among the environment which is observed in many universities today. Learning in the groups may consist of students from different cultures and hence multicultural participants. Many scholars have discussed the issues of multicultural learning environment that cannot be avoided in today's HE (Manathunga (2009, 20017), Herd & Moore (2012), Thomas, Chinn, Perkins, & Carter (1994)). Thus, students in a group meet with diverse ethics, but they must integrate theirs and the new cultures regardless of their backgrounds. Students themselves are accountable for the creation of a conducive learning environment that suits all cultures and members. They can do this by making group rules to observe or providing equal opportunities to demonstrate their culture. Learning in such a multicultural environment tends to create an inclusive mind-set, which is vital in the learning environment, workplaces, and real life.

Disadvantages of Collaborative Learning

Indeed, collaborative learning requires adequate democracy compared to the limited time students may have. It is mostly democracy that facilitates collaborative learning decisions. The discussion and collaborative decision-making process consume time, and that to reach a conclusion can be a challenging experience. There is no way one student will make decisions for a group all the time (although sometimes this can happen). Without a doubt, there are several decisions to be made in a collaborative learning environment. Sometimes this kind of democratic decision-making process takes time for the participants to reach the desired common ground. For example, a group of six students who are required to solve an academic task on, let us say, a child abuse topic, group members may have different preferences about when to study and where to meet, and even how to discuss the topic. If three of them have shared preferences about the venue, the other two must compromise. If they are not professional and democratic enough to cope with the choice of others and give way to democracy, it might be a challenge for them to cooperate. Therefore, the dissatisfaction situation may even affect the way members contribute to the group.

Domination and Bias

Sometimes collaborative learning can lead to a division of members. For instance, there is a tendency for some students' suggestions to be considered more important than others in a group. There are diverse reasons for this favouritism; sometimes, it might be caused by language, experiences, and even culture. Thus, when the suggestions of some members get their way and if this frequently happens to the same students, it may affect the way others contribute to the group. Sometimes, some students, especially whose choice are not getting anywhere, tend to feel ignored and invisible. Although their thoughts and feelings are sometimes genuine and need attention, they are not attended to, creating division in a group and unnecessary misunderstandings that affect the cooperation.

Furthermore, in collaborative learning, a few students may dominate the group and press forth their ideas with less priority to observe ideas from other group members. In such a situation, a group leader should ensure order where each member contributes to his best. For example, it might be by assigning small tasks from the significant task to every member and compile their contributions in one way or the other. Or ask fundamental questions about the topic and contributions sequentially. Undeniably, without order, some students may be shadowed by others with strong personalities and unwilling to learn from others.

Moreover, assessment procedures can lead to domination. There is a kind of collaborative learning where the students receive the same grades in the group assignment. For example, the assignments in a group where students collaborate and contribute to finding a solution and acquire the same grades may be destructive. For example, one or more students can present the assignment without contribution from others, and everyone in the group obtains the same grade regardless of their absence. Sometimes, this kind of assessment is against demonstrating individual contributions and ability. Often, such an assessment procedure allows few students to work harder than others and receive the same grades as those who were less engaged. If the group receives good grades, the contributors tend to dominate the group for further assignments and ignore other members' contributions.

Previous Experiences

Group members tend to have different experiences. Their experiences may affect their understanding and contribution to the topic in question. There are some principles to be considered without judgmental thoughts, actions, and attitudes when dealing with a group. This process of evaluating other peoples' ideas needs a higher understanding and respect of each other's points of view. For example, let us go back to the child abuse topic; the members' contributions can have "north and south poles." The participants in the group may discuss the topic using personal experiences, especially if they have experienced abuse in their childhood or know of someone's experience. Indeed, in the discussion, some participants may feel like a therapy session whilst discussing their experiences, and others may feel overwhelmed, leading to unpleasant and discomfort experiences. Therefore, in such a situation, the group members ought to respect these diverging experiences and even learn from them.

Likewise, it might happen that the participants have heard diverse stories about child abuse, which are contrary to their perspective. The diverging perception may also be part of the conversation and can happen if the cultures of the group participants are different. The members may have different viewpoints about the abuse that need more time to discuss and comprehend or include in the assignment. No surprise that not all abusive actions western scholars write in their publications are translated similarly by every culture. Therefore, group members can have diverse perspectives based on their cultural backgrounds that influence their perceptions and need to be understood. However, such diverse thoughts and cultures may be an advantage for students in adjusting their thoughts and respect others through discussions that are free from judgment.

Therefore, strategies applied in leading a group are vital in HE learning. Thus, collaboration may facilitate group learning or hinder some students from participating fully, depending on how the process undergo and decisions are made. Nevertheless, a group leader should moderate the group learning process, decision-making, and sometimes the ruling can be conducted against democracy to better the group members' contributions.

Diverse Opinions about the Learning Styles

As a result, these two kinds of learning styles (individual and collaborative) can also demonstrate students' skills. The students' activities become different in individual and group learning. Even the practices are different depending on the contexts (physical or digital) and the content. There are some positive and negative effects that students should observe in each learning style, as discussed. For example, I asked students what learning style they preferred; some said they preferred cooperative learning. Nonetheless, they were not ready to work in a group with whoever and whatever situation. On the contrary, the majority preferred to work with people they knew from before because they think they can contribute without tension when working with strangers.

Indeed, some students feared unknown people and strangers. Those who supported the idea of working with familiar people in a group suggested that working with strangers is a time-consuming business because students sometimes need to be comfortable with each other's values before tackling academic tasks. They believed that understanding and being familiar with each other values and beliefs that the members hold dearly may facilitate discussion positively. Some pointed out the gender and sexual orientation and other issues related to religious beliefs that can be harmful to discuss with whoever, and whatever issues. For those students, collaborative learning is beneficial only when all group members understand each other's values and beliefs before solving academic tasks together.

Other students thought that group work in HE is beneficial when all members comprehend what to do. The task should be straightforward for the group members to engage actively; otherwise, if only a few grasp what should be done, some may become followers. Students pointed out the challenges some students face concerning the language of instruction and how it hinders their understanding of the requirements. The students emphasized that understanding the assignment is vital for creating equal opportunity in students' contribution. When all members know the assignment's requirements and can solve the problem, it may lead to a high chance of being equally valued in the group. Indeed, if factors that lead to equal opportunities in a group will not be considered, collaborative learning can be the agent of dishonesty, disharmony, and an unsafe learning environment.

Despite the diverse arguments about collective learning shortfalls, some students and academics agreed that the collaborative learning method is vital. They believe this method could bring solutions to many challenges faced by HE, and many societies. They consider that today's global problems need collaborative viewpoints in finding solutions. Moreover, HEIs are observing the increased multicultural environments, and societies are facing the same situation. So, it has been challenging to have an environment free from diverse cultures, thoughts, and belief patterns. Therefore, they think that students can learn different ways of solving problems when working collaboratively with others with different values. By doing so, they learn from others, and above all, they tend to build a strong network. Indeed, most world's problems need solutions from diverse sources and people of all backgrounds who can work collaboratively and constructively.

Likewise, students who favoured collaboration believed that some of the networks that emerged in HE learning groups have lifelong importance. They believed that these networks might lead to employment after their graduation, either local or global. For example, a group of students found out from one member that the government (in his country) needed some teachers to teach specific languages. This information was delivered to them by the student who was a group member. Most of the students in the group were linguistics, and some applied for jobs they heard about and received an offer. However, the offer was conditioned to the students' successful graduates. One student, Shasa,

155

asserted: *"I am very thankful to be offered a job even before graduation. I could not know this if my co-group member did not inform me about the vacancy. I am very excited to live abroad. I am finding a network, and I am also reading more about the country's culture because I will start the job in five months if everything goes well."* The students who had job offers were thankful for the group work that connected her with the informant. Indeed, some groups' networks create lifelong connections that lead to family, career, and job opportunities.

A Statement of Warning

For information, collaborative learning is not an arena for competition neither contradiction. The students must be aware of how the group works to reduce competition and enhance collaboration. Sometimes, it might be challenging to identifying individual effort within a group if the group leader is not skilful or the assignment is not well constructed to measure individual participation. Nevertheless, the benefits associated with collaborative learning are equally important as those obtained from individual learning. However, each style develops different skills and produces different knowledge. One should determine the skills he desires to develop or acquire before choosing the learning context (physical or online) or judging which kind is more beneficial. In addition, these learning styles (collaboratively or individually) may be more beneficial if they are applied interchangeably to facilitate diverse skills acquisition.

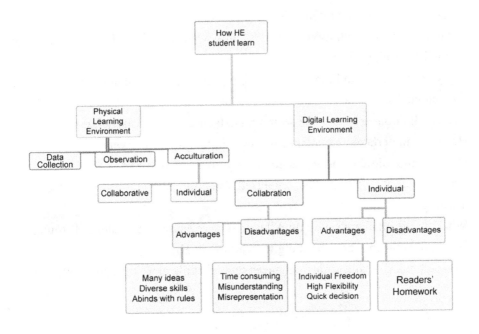

Figure 8. The physical and Digital Learning Model

Learning in higher education is complex but comprehensive. Currently, most students choose two major approaches thus: physical and online. In physical learning, students learn through observation, acculturation, and data collection individually or collaboratively. Another approach is digital learning, where students learn online without physical contact with learning agencies and institutions. Digital learning can also be arranged to cater to individual needs or a group. Indeed, both approaches have merits and demerits one should evaluate before commencing the degree studies. The ones indicated in figure-eight are examples people have experienced based on their perceptions of these approaches, and their approach may differ from the information you obtain after your investigation.

Self-Reflection

What is your level of computer skills?

Are you familiar with diverse computer programs? Explain.

What is your favourite referencing digital program?

What are your searching web pages, and what kind of information do you normally search for?

Are you aware of the kind of referencing programs applied at the university of your choice?

Are you familiar with diverse searching databases for scholarly literature?

Have you undertaken any course through digital devices? Explain.

Do you think digital learning is good for you? Explain.

How can digital learning be organised for both individual and collaborative learning?

What are the challenges you think learners may encounter in digital learning?

What are your opinions about digital learning in HE?

Do you think digital learning enhances several skills more than physical learning?

Chapter IX
Challenges in Higher Education Learning

There are many challenges in HE learning environment today. Even the changes mentioned in the previous chapters are among the problems faced by HE. I propose that all the changes discussed in the previous chapters are challenges HEIs encounter. For example, the change from HE "for the elite" to "all" creates challenges of learning spaces, materials, and educators (McAlpine & Amundsen (2012), Posselt, Abdelkafi, Fischer, & Tangour (2019). Changes from uni-culture learning environments to multicultural contexts have created challenges between educators, students, and other agencies in communication and expectations (Grant & Manathunga (2011), Lee (2007)).

Likewise, the change from less involvement of states in HE to vigorous involvement and control (Kiley (2011), Maassen et al. (2004), MoENZ (2015), Stensaker et al. (2008), Stensaker (2006)) has created challenges in learning and supervision of students. In addition, the situation has led to the implementation of governmental and institutional policies that sometimes, according to scholars, jeopardise students learning. Again, the shift of focus by most universities from public service, knowledge provider, to the business profit-maker organisation through knowledge economy is also a problem (Kostrykina et al. (2017), Van Der Wende (2015)). As a result, the majority need to purchase education at high prices involving monetary, social, cultural, and emotional aspects.

I do not desire to repeat what I have mentioned in the previous chapter about changes in HE to make you see how problematic these changes threat students' learning. Instead, I want you to understand that the challenges are the first guests to appear whenever there is a change. Therefore, I will discuss some of the disputes that most scholars have observed and that these changes persist from the traditional era of HE to the modern era. Even if the extent to which these issues affect the modern HE may differ from the traditional, still, they are obstacles for students' learning.

Gender Differences

There is a pedagogical challenge related to gender in HE. I discussed how the female was disadvantaged in the traditional era of HE and that education was mostly for young males. Although both female and male students have access to HE today, practically female students are still disadvantaged. The majority have huge responsibilities in their families that hinder them from taking advantage of their resources in HE (Lindsey, 2015). In addition, some women experience discrimination in HE learning environment through their learning agencies. For example, Lee (2007) asserted that HE matured female students often feel abandoned even with their supervisors than their male counterparts. This act of discrimination in the learning environment might be observed in many universities and is probably grounded on the historical background of women's roles. Still, some people think that women who join HE interfere with men's positions and hence pay less attention to female academic needs.

Certainly, females, in some universities, tend to receive different treatment compared to male students. Therefore, learning environment might be complicated for female students, and that they have little information on how to obtain and demand the service they deserve (Lindsey, 2015). Female students have a lot to do before they reach the same ladder as male students in some learning environments, because they are not considered equal. The literature has also shown that most female students tend to have different demands in HE learning from male students (Carter, Blumenstein, & Cook, 2013), and their partnership with the learning agencies such as supervisors tends to be different, especially when a supervisor is of the opposite sex. Connell and Manathunga (2012) described bad practices provided with supervision in the traditional era, such as sexual exploitation of students. This problem has been mentioned by another scholar, Grant (2003, 2008, 2011), in the modern era. Therefore, people who desire to join HE and female students should consider dealing with such conduct.

The issue of gender differences in HE has been observed by other scholars too. Some have expressed their concern about different practices and perspectives on gender in HE. For example, Bell-Ellison and Dedrick (2008), Lindsey (2015), Evans and Waring (2011) demonstrated divergence in pedagogical preferences and cognitive perception between male and female students that call for attention. Their different preferences should be known by learning agencies who desire to support students. This is vital in creating effective communication, understanding, and respecting female students' perspectives and needs in the learning environment. One of the differences between male and female students mentioned by other researchers (Carter et al. (2013), Johansson, Wisker, Claesson, Strandler, & Saalman (2014)) is that most female students consider HE learning as an emotional journey, while male counterparts have a different perspective about learning in HE. In another study on the ideal mental scale, females desired the learning agencies with higher integrity (respect for self and others) than guidance capabilities (Bethany A. Bell-Ellison & Robert F. Dedrick, 2008).

Therefore, it is challenging to supervise students, especially female students with different expectations from males, without discussing their needs. For example, two supervisors informed me that some mature female students are not active in social events conducted at their institution compared to their male counterparts in real life. They also inform that they slip up some informal learning through interaction with others by not participating in those events. One supervisor asserted: *"Some social events connect both students and faculties, and both parties tend to discuss, in a relaxed manner, some crucial issues that can be beneficial for students in their learning. However, female students' absence in these gatherings may isolate them from the rest of the students' community and faculty"*. Another supervisor added: *"These students isolate themselves even when we desire to include them in diverse activities."* Thus, the gender difference is a useful message to mature female students who want to join HE or those already enrolled. The information can also support female students to integrate with others by participating in possible university campus activities as is required. The significant point is to avoid isolation and interacting with peers and other vital people and ideas that can benefit their study and future career. Even if one has a stable career, she might create a useful network to share her experiences and even enjoy and make herself known.

This information about mature female isolation may be observed in other sectors too. The supervisors' information reminds me of the research I conducted in 1998 in the bachelor's degree where female students' physical education/activities were deteriorating at one university. It was a challenge to convince female students to utilise the training facilities in the university's training centre. I applied the quantitative research method to find out the reason behind female absentees in physical activities. In addition, I was interested in finding the frequency of female students' attendance at the gymnastics centre and other physical activities arenas on the campus. I employed a survey questionnaire followed by interviews with a few female students and some physical activity coordinators.

The results indicated that most female students who had family responsibilities had no time for physical activities in the evening. They were interested in exercising and being healthy, but many responsibilities tied them out of the training services. Even though they were aware of the benefits physical exercises could bring, such as stimulating creativity, increasing focus on learning, and keeping them healthy (Siedentop, Hastie, & Van der Mars (2019), still, they could not attend. Students had family responsibilities and several other tasks in the evening, simultaneously when the centres were open.

Therefore, HE female situation is still different from most males and requires extra attention to optimise their learning opportunities. More researchers and training are required to understand issues related to gender and females learning in HE. Even some female faculties encounter challenges associated with gender role stereotypes. Likewise, LaPan, Hodge, Peroff, and Henderson's (2013) study indicated that female HE teachers face three types of challenges. First, the politics of HE, like all other faculties associated with changes mentioned earlier, the politics of gender because they are female, and the politics of family caring as the stereotype role expected of females.

Indeed, more research is required to investigate issues related to gender and females. Although female and gender issues have become imbalanced for a long time, few researchers have investigated and documented gender issues in HE and challenges females encounter in academics. For example, even when Pla-Julian and Diez (2019) conducted gender perception research at a Spanish university, they found no clear perception of gender issues and gender equality. Likewise, the European Commission report on gender equality in academia indicated the underrepresentation of women in some disciplines and even gender researchers.

Formally, Lovas (1980) asserted:

"Women are clearly disadvantaged but some of the reasons may be those not usually seen as discriminatory. They appear to be restricted by the operation of three factors in addition to those usually said to operate against women. A high proportion…, they may also have limited access to publication opportunities in overseas journals and are more frequently found in arts-type disciplines." (p. 8).

One might think that this information is old and not applicable in our time. However, although provided almost three decades ago, I am afraid Lovas' statement is the reality of females' current situation in some HEIs. The same trend was currently observed by Pla-Julian and Diez (2019), who mentioned that most students and academics in agricultural science, natural science, technology, and engineering are male. This situation is the evidence of the persistence of inequality and calls for equality plans and integration of gender perspectives in HE learning and practices. Likewise, gender policies formulation may also facilitate the positive gender perspective and equality by introducing specific education about gender differences, equality, and benefits. Indeed, a discussion leading to understanding the challenges of gender may also be beneficial for people who desire to join HE. As a result, it may lead to thinking to write and research on the topic.

Now, you know that gender inequality exists in HE, and that needs scientific investigation and knowledge. Well, you may GO FOR IT, be a problem solver, research about it, and share the findings.

Diverse Evaluation Procedures

Diversity in degree programmes has led to different assessment criteria that are considered among the challenges HEIs encounter. It has been difficult to standardise the assessment procedures, the results, and the quality of higher education (EURASHE (European Ministers in charge of Higher Education), 2016) even within a country, the university, and the department. Most universities are practicing, learning differently, and they usually focus on both local and global demands so as the assessment. For example, in most Commonwealth universities, writing is critical, and some examiners do not require oral examinations. While in New Zealand, the UK, and the Scandinavian countries (Braathe & Otterstad (2014), Kelly, (2010)), oral examinations are equally important as written examinations for students in their process of learning and completing a degree. For the institutions that conduct oral examinations, the primary purpose has been to ensure the student acquiring the degree can communicate his knowledge. The oral examination allows a student to discuss his work in depth while examiners evaluate whether the student's presentation and understanding is based on his written work. In this case, the student's writing, communication, and other skills are measured simultaneously.

Likewise, there is a variation in examiners' involvement. For example, some universities, especially in Europe and some Commonwealth countries, involve external examiners in students' summative evaluation (Sheehan, 1994). At the same time, other countries do not have this kind of external academics' involvement in students' assessment. Sometimes, this procedure can create anxiety, especially for students who originate from the evaluation system without external examiners. For example, if a doctoral student had no external examiner from the previous learning environment; bachelor, and master's degree, it might be challenging to meet with such experience at the doctoral level. However, information about this practice in advance, can support the students in preparation.

Undoubtedly, the formative and summative evaluation information and its procedures need to be conveyed to applicants to support them in selecting an institution. People may choose which assessment practices they prefer and whether they favour the institutions, which involves internal and external examiners or the opposite. It is not enough for universities to explain the courses, examination time, and complaint procedures without mentioning the assessment procedures (Lovas, 1980). Such information may seem insignificant to some people, but according to my informants, it is a big issue that causes a high level of stress when revealed late in their studies. I cannot emphasise enough how vital it is to inform applicants about the assessment procedures in-depth for their decision and preparation.

Indeed, people need to understand the whole assessment process because it is the key to failure or success. Some scholars have discussed the issue of HE students' assessment (Golding et al. (2014), Wisker & Robinson (2014)), and the knowledge in these scholarly writings can support stakeholders in their choice and preparation. For instance, universities may convey information about how many examiners will be involved in the formative and summative evaluation and what students expect in the assessment. The information can support people in their choice and preparation before enrolment. For instance, if someone is uncomfortable with the external examination system, he can opt for the institution which does not practice such a procedure and vice versa. Therefore, I recommend people seek for adequate information about assessment before heading to a university.

Bullying in Higher Education

The higher education learning environment is not as conducive as it should be. Although we have heard about bullying acts in lower levels of education, it should not be taboo to discuss bullying in HE. Some universities have seen the necessity of examining the psychosocial learning environment of HE students and call for an investigation, as Lund and Ross (2017) recommended. The investigation is vital because bullying is not affecting people only in the period they face it, but the effect of bullying can persist for a lifetime (Young-Jones, Fursa, Byrket, & Sly, 2015). It is no surprise that people who have experienced bullying in lower levels of education can be the victim or bullies at higher levels. Even though the majority think that students in HE are mature and able to resist the actions of bullies, in reality, no one is mature for bullying, and the effects of bullying affect everyone involved. Avoiding discussing bullying in HE is not healthy, but understanding its existence and its effect may be beneficial for creating a conducive psychosocial learning environment.

Few scholarly literatures has discussed bullying in HE. Most scholars have emphasized their investigation in lower levels of education. However, some measures to prevent and reduce bullying at the secondary level of education can be applied in tertiary education. According to the report provided by the Centre for Learning Environment in Stavanger, Norway (CLES), (2017) titled "Bullying in different nations," the report disclosed the findings in bullying investigation conducted using survey questionnaires, which involved secondary schools in 40 countries. The researchers focused on finding out students' experiences about bullying acts and their involvement in bullying. The results indicated that 10.7% of the adolescents had acted like bullies, 12.6% as victims, and 3.6% had been victims and bullies. Therefore, the result indicated that most students learn in an unpleasant environment full of bullies and bullying acts.

Researchers believe that there are reasons behind all sorts of bullying. For example, some asserted that bullying is probably a mental health problem, and those involved in bullying activities call for help. Furthermore, they believe that they choose bullying strategy because bullies have lost trust in humans and manipulate and display dishonest and distrust behaviour (Whitney & Smith (1993), Young-Jones, Fursa, Byrket & Sly (2015)). Likewise, scholars and parents blame the education system, allowing isolation, discrimination, and exclusion of some groups in the learning environments (Chambers, 2011). These explanations cause me to consider bullying as a major challenge in education and

HE. Therefore, sharing information about bullying is vital to support HE stakeholders to re-examine the education system and initiate measures to cover the existing loophole for bullies.

Certainly, some gaps in formal education facilitate bullying at different levels. For example, most institutions isolate extra curriculum (physical activities, sports, and social events) from their core curriculum and that students' attendance at these activities might be optional and on their own time and expenses. Because it is optional, some students do not prioritise and have neither time nor money to attend these essential extra curriculum activities. Most of the activities require self-motivation, and some students lack the discipline required for participation. Lack of students' association with others out of formal academic programmes minimises their opportunity to demonstrate their talents and other values. Refer to the issue of female students' association discussed by supervisors in the gender section. Students' lack of participation in extra-curriculum activities, where they could demonstrate their non-academic talents, limit their creativity and mental wellbeing. One student Andria, commented: *"To most young people, the lack of arena for show off of their non-academic capacities may lead to frustration, and hence they may compensate their disappointments with the destructive actions."* I am not legitimating this behavior, where people should seek attention through destructive activities, but policymakers and institution management should pay more attention to this factor.

The system of education needs to accommodate students' talents and values outside the classroom. The system cannot assume that their parents or peers will support students to access extra-curricular activities, including social events and sports. Some students who have no sports arenas, for example, often experience isolation. One informant, John, described how he engaged in bullying activities:

"I was not chosen to be one of the players on the basketball team in school, the sport which was my favourite. I was very good at basketball, but I had some differences with the trainer. As a result, I could not find a suitable activity or group that could accommodate me for extra-curriculum activities. I tried to be with other students. I thought we could have something in common, but I realized they were against me. I felt miserable and frustrated because nothing was for me. I had no activity after academics or reliable friends whom I could trust and hang out together. Therefore, I started using verbal assaults on other students and

troubled others, including my teachers, out of frustration. It went on like that for some months where I got into one problem to the other.

All bullies have some background information that can justify their practices, but all in all-ins a lack of guidance and training to be a good person. When someone does wrong, most people tend to run away from the person than cooperate to discover the challenges the person encounters. The more people run from the bullies, the more they strength their behaviour, instead, people need to come closer to consult the person in finding a solution.

John continued: *luckily, one day, one of my favourite teachers had a long conversation with me, asking why I was engaging in trouble. I managed to inform about my frustration and experiences, including the bias among teachers which was going on. The teacher listened to me, and finally, he asked me what I was interested in doing as extra-curriculum activity. I informed him that I like working with balls and on computers, technically. Immediately, he picked the phone and contacted a computer department to find out whether they had any project where I could be part of it. Fortunately, the computer coordinator in the department was looking for students who could join a pivotal group as students' computer assistants where students could get support whenever they have a problem with their computer for little payment. It was an appropriate timing, so I joined the group and learned how to respect people and provide better services as a computer assistant. I have attended several courses where respect and integrity are discussed. Since my engagement with computer project, I had no time for bullying activities anymore,"* The student (the informant) added: *"I realized most bullies lack a better way of utilising their time and energy. Sometimes they have unutilised resources that need to be discovered and put into work, like me."* His explanations make me believe that bullies need help and that blaming and discriminating against them can make things worse.

The story aligns with what scholars (Whitney & Smith (1993), Young-Jones et al. (2015)) indicated that most bullies intend to search for power, security, masculinity, and even material gain. It is believed that some bullies desire to express their emotional illness without being understood. Educational institutions often create an ambiguous situation for students, as I mentioned earlier.

Even when students call for such attention, less attention in school and at home may lead to destructive behavior. Scholars believe that some students' crying for help does not reach their parents, teachers, curriculum developers, problem solvers, or policymakers (Spriggs, Iannotti, Nansel, & Haynie, 2007). Most academics and civilians believe that institutions have more responsibility to reduce and eradicate bullying as they are with students longer than parents/guardians (except for holidays). However, the collaboration between the educational institutions and families is essential in attending learners' calls. Although these scholars investigated the schooling in lower levels, their findings might apply to HE.

Nevertheless, there is no guarantee that bullying will be over with the curriculum and extra-curricular participation. Different perspectives facilitate the actions; for example, some students think bullying others is a fun game due to, among others, cultural background or their upbringing. The Centre for Learning Environment in Stavanger (2017) reported it mentioned negative parenting styles among the causes of bullying. Most parents and guardians have a more stressful lifestyle today than ever before, where children's needs are unattended and children have little supervision. The absence of parental guidance, supervision, and care has made some children learn from other sources such as media information. As a result, the online information about life and youth can be destructive or wrongly translated, especially if the youth does not have any guidance to translate it correctly.

Likewise, most parents have little time to cooperate with learning institutions. Although they desire to be part of a learning institution and support teachers and pay attention to their children's daily challenges, they are unaware of the benefits associated with this involvement (Spriggs et al., 2007). Most children are probably longing for such attention and involvement from their parents. When they do not get what they want, they tend to engage in destructive acts, and bullying can be one of the alternatives. The scholars proclaimed:

"Children may hit, exclude, or harass others electronically because when their own needs for belongingness are threatened, or when they want to enhance their own status, they lash out and hurt others in the way they think will be more painful, by engaging in behaviours that undermine the target's sense of belongingness" (Spriggs et al., 2007 p. 1).

Again, this can be observed clearly in lower levels of education, but it is even more important for an individual to acquire attention and to belong somewhere when learning in HE. Therefore, families, friends, and peers are vital for HE students' success, and they need support to modify their behavior accordingly. Of course, not all students will be lucky to be accommodated in a meaningful project in HE like John, but working with teachers, family, peers, and friends can be beneficial.

Sometimes, bullying behaviour grows with individual growth. Although I cannot point out research verifying this belief, I strongly believe that people who were bullies in secondary schools without facing negative consequences for their actions, may tend to behave in the same way in HE. For example, I heard of this male high school student who was a member of the students' parliament. He was not comfortable sitting in the parliament with one female student at all. So, he used different techniques to harass her, and one time he even wrote her a letter using toilet paper to intimidate her. The troubles were that the female student was brighter than the male student, which was not what he desired. The female student was appointed to the students' government, and she questioned some issues male students were practicing in the parliament and demanded some changes. The male members of the students' government scored her and bulled her openly and everywhere.

In fact, in the 1990s, ordinarily female students received not much support from the institutions when they were bullied in many parts of the world. Similarly, one boy in the parliament continued with harassment to the female student and did not receive any consequence for his actions, even when the female student reported several bullying incidences. When the male student joined HE for a degree, the same young man was elected a representative for science students in the university's students' union due to, among others, his charismatic behavior. Having power as the representative and his bullying experience made him a dangerous person to other students (especially females) and academics. I heard he could not graduate because he finally got fired for a brutal bullying act he committed. His story is one of the many that made me conclude that a bully's behaviour may be transferred from one level of education to the other if bullies do not receive help and negative reinforcement.

The Consequences of Bullying

It is hard to ignore the effect of bullying on individuals. One of the severe consequences is suicidal thoughts for both parties (Young-Jones et al., 2015). The bullies and victims might reach a point to end their lives in one way or another, based on guilt and shame. Indeed, bullying creates a sense of intimidation and shame so, the victims may desire to end their lives and not continue with existence. In other cases, students who have experienced bullying tend to become passive with lower academic motivation and avoidance of learning context and learning agencies. They may postpone contact with supervisors, peers, friends, and even family members, depending on the nature of the bullying act they experienced. Likewise, bullies tend to be disappointed because they usually obtain unexpected and unprepared attention that sometimes frightens them.

For example, Physical bullying for those who have experienced it tends to create fear. The victims may fear other people around them to the extent of failing to communicate or contact others physically or face to face (Cassell (2011), Young-Jones et al. (2015)). The victim may fear being alone or even speaking their mind to people around them. Such behavior can affect students in a group discussion where they may fear conveying their views and making mistakes. Likewise, it is believed that physical bullying harms the victim, including inclinations, a long-term feeling of insecurity, and holds negative perspectives toward themselves and others. In the research I mentioned earlier from Norway, secondary school children's experiences concerning physical bullying might be different from HE experiences. However, people should remember that physical bullying exists in HE learning environments (Connell & Manathunga, 2012), although it might be in different forms, such as sexual abuse.

Currently, students in HE have experienced another bullying through technology. For example, in cyberbullying, the victims tend to withdraw themselves from social media and other technological communication channels and prefer physical contact or no contact at all (Hinduja & Patchin (2010), Lund & Ross (2017). Currently, we are witnessing bullying through social media and the internet every day when we read news and other information. People of all backgrounds observe bullying and that calls for severe measures to fight against cyberbullying. Educational institutions and families have a lot to teach their members how to communicate on social media and handle information on the internet. In the education context, when students or academics experience cyberbullying, it is destructive because learning in, HE needs the connection of learners with different learning agencies through digital mediums. Those who have experienced bullying on social media tend to isolate themselves from the media, and by so doing, they miss vital information and networking required of them in higher education.

Indeed, no matter the level of education, gender, position, and other personal attributes, bullying affects individual development negatively. For instance, a study conducted by Carol et al. (2011) on cyberbullying in HE found that the victims of cyberbullying (through Facebook, YouTube, and other internet programme channels) tend to feel long-lasting anger and unhappiness regardless of their background. Likewise, the study conducted in a Finnish university in 2010, found that 5% of 2805 students, who responded to the digital questionnaires, admitted experiencing either indirect public physical bullying or direct oral bullying (Hanna et al. 2012) and that students had to either drop out or avoid contact with bullies. In addition, the study indicated the victims experienced psychological problems, lack of learning, motivation, weakening of self-confidence, low learning capability, and depression.

In Norway, the report provided by Lund and Ross (2017) regards bullying indicated that it has a severe barrier in post-secondary learning. These researchers examined 14 studies where 20–25% of students experienced non-cyber bullying and 10–15% experienced cyberbullying harassment in HE learning. Almost 20% of students committed non-cyber bullying, and about 5% is reported cyber perpetration. Likewise, Lund (2017) indicated that 71% of HE students had experienced psychological bullying, 41% verbal, 4% digital, and 3% experienced physical bullying. The information demonstrates a severe problem of bullying in HE learning environments. Therefore, HE applicants and learners ought to have strategies to recognise bullying activities and become aware of how to tackle this challenge in advance. Students should understand the procedures to follow in case they face bullying situations and try to avoid the circumstances that may lead them to be bullies to others.

Bullying Catalysts

Several things accelerate bullying actions. First, the sophisticated development of technology and its accessibility quickened cyberbullying (Li (2006), Slonje & Smith (2008)). Students have access to technology and the internet twenty-four-seven, and they can click anywhere without thinking. Second, using technology is supported by a conspiracy of false news and manipulating pictures and images (Barratt-Pugh & Krestelica (2018), Cassell (2011), Keashly & Neuman (2013)). Third, there are many loopholes that bullies utilising to oppress their victims psychologically and emotionally using technology. Fourth, bullies have no respect for a person; we have observed in different online news where people with high positions and status in the societies are attacked badly by bullies, most of the time, without apparent reason. Finally, manipulating information destroys the reality of the issue and the truth about the person, just as McCornack, (2015) discussed. Therefore, cyberbullies have made it difficult to separate the truth, and fake information about issues and people.

Likewise, HE's multicultural learning environment is believed to accelerate bullying actions (Grant & Mckinley (2011), Grant (2008)). The mixture of students and academics from diverse backgrounds and desperate seeking for belonging strengthen the challenges (Grant & Mckinley (2011), Grant (2005), Grant (2008)). The mixing of cultures by itself may bring tension to the well-being of participants. There are different experiences people describe when meeting with foreign cultures, which can create a bullying arena. As I mentioned earlier, students come from diverse backgrounds with biased beliefs associated with race, religion, gender, and age. When they come together, these diverse faiths may result in an uncomfortable situation that may create a bullying situation. To avoid bullying, students need to understand that the way they think and believe is not always the only and right way rather a part of multiple thoughts and values.

Indeed, there are many bullying agencies; however, I would instead leave this to you to evaluate your learning environment. One principle is that every person in HE should be responsible for creating the environment they desire by respecting different thoughts and values that are different from theirs. It might be difficult for institutions to create a perfect learning environment, but teaching the fundamental principle of respect should lead to HE learning. In collaboration with their learning agencies, students should participate freely and fully in creating the environment they desire by observing what is lawful from the beginning of their learning. Furthermore, students and academics may create rules vital for pleasant learning regardless of policymakers and institutions' management. Students and academics need to create a common ground, which respects and integrates cultures, values, and ideas from all backgrounds without jeopardising individual freedom, well-being, values, and learning. Unfortunately, bullying is a challenge that has persisted in educational institutions from lower levels to universities, and that requires a collaborative effort to eradicate it. Therefore, everyone must prepare for and demonstrate good conduct that opposes bullying and enhance learning for all.

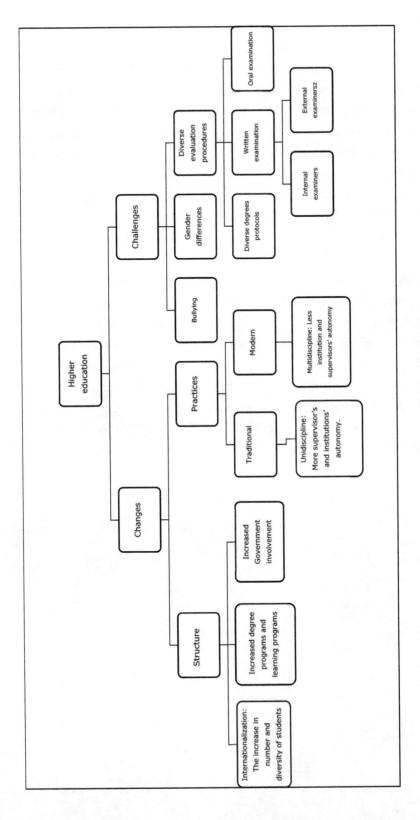

Figure 9. Changes and Challenges HE Practitioners Encounter

Figure 9 indicates that the higher education learning system has changed and has several challenges one must comprehend before commencing. First, the change has affected the structure and practices that have resulted in internationalization, which facilitates student movement and increases in northern and western universities, increasing degree programs and government involvement. Second, the practice has change leading to vivid differences between the traditional and modern learning practices. The third is the difference between an elite education system and mass education for all who meet the criteria. The fourth is the change from uni-culture and monodisciplinary to the multicultural and multidisciplinary learning environment.

Moreover, there are several challenges higher education practitioners encounter. Most of them are bullying, gender differences, and complex evaluation procedures. For example, in assessment, in some universities, students are required to write their theses and defend them through the oral presentation, while in others, the written document is the only part of the examination. Indeed, one must comprehend different challenges associated with these two types of assessments to avoid obstacles that may hinder their performance. In addition, some universities have not formulated measures that may hinder bullying in their institutions. Therefore, they must consider communicating bullying incidences, their origin, and effects for students to comprehend and fight against.

Self-Reflection

What do you think are big challenges in HE?

Do you think gender equality is important to be investigated and considered? Explain.

What do you think can facilitate gender inequality?

What measures are to be taken to promote gender equality in HE?

Do you think diverse students' evaluation creates the problem of identifying their skills? Explain.

What kind of bullying acts have you experienced?

How to eradicate bullying in HE psychosocial learning environments?

Do you understand the procedures to be taken in cases of bullying in your institution?

What kind of employment do you expect after graduation?

What skills do you think you possess that might lead to employment?

What is your opinion of graduates concerning employment?

What do you think employers should do to identify qualified graduates?

The Conclusion

I am happy that I have informed the fundamental practices that exist in HE. The diversities and opportunities which exist in current HEIs practices have not been observed before. It is believed that this is the movement time where nothing stands still, so do knowledge and HE structure and practices. Indeed, some perceive changes in HE as the obstacles to quality learning, and others embrace the changes as an opportunity for knowledge utilisation and cooperation. Similarly, although there is an increased number and diversity of HE participants, some people find it challenging to join HE because knowledge is everywhere and no longer bound in the hands of formal learning institutions. So, diverse perspectives need to be considered and investigated concerning the legitimacy and benefits of HE individually and cooperatively. There is no doubt that HEIs management and other stakeholders have changed their practices but face numerous challenges in this modern era of abundant knowledge and the knowledge economy.

Likewise, a comparison between the old days and the modern days is discussed in this book. The information is vital to consider before commencing HE as it highlights diverse practices and requirements. Such discussion is vital to support people with adequate information for preparation. Likewise, the book explains the change from elite and service-oriented HE to mass and business knowledge economy. Again, change from uni-culture and undisciplined to multicultural and multidiscipline learning environments.

Moreover, the discussion includes altering students' completion time from flexible and the goddess of supervisors to fixed and limited completion time with powerless supervisors. In addition, the old era was the era of academics and institutional empowerments while governments were less involved, but governments are the vital HE stakeholder with financial power in the modern era. Therefore, the information in this book is a part of discussions and investigations that can benefit higher education stakeholders, especially students and academics, who can extend the debate and work with the topics in this book in many ways. Otherwise, anyone who desires to acquire a degree needs to know this book's mentioned changes and challenges to succeed.

Moreover, as a reader, if you intend to join HE or have enrolled in a university, I believe this information will guide you in better comprehending the practices in your institution. Likewise, I have conveyed information about how learning is organised, the different styles and forms of learning, and the fundamental learning content in HE for more preparation. Indeed, I discuss the learning content to support readers in evaluating their needs and ensuring the acquisition of the knowledge they expected and required upon graduation. The information is vital for individuals to evaluate their preferences while investigating the knowledge and skills, including the institutional practices, in advance. Unquestionably, one needs to understand why he needs a degree, what is going on in HEIs, and the learning challenges.

Preparation is always the key to the success of any human plan, including education. Therefore, one must prepare for both individual and cooperative learning, and that the book discusses both forms and their merits. Indeed, digital and physical learning styles develop and enhance graduates' different skills, and many institutions combine the two. Therefore, knowing the knowledge and skills one benefits from these learning styles is essential for the individual to formulate strategies to participate and motivate himself. Thus, comprehending the skills acquired from HE learning before graduation can enhance graduates' confidence when collaborating with others in problem-solving in real life.

I believe that what I have discussed from the reasons people desire a degree, the traditional and modern higher education practices are vital. Likewise, information about learning theories, contents, styles, and challenges that HE stakeholders encounter will support many unaware of the current HEIs' situations. However, the information is a drop of water in the ocean, meaning is little information compared to the demand from HE stakeholders. More information is needed to educate and support stakeholders in their decisions and efforts to eradicate HE challenges. Without a doubt, HEIs and stakeholders face several challenges, especially in this era of coronavirus, that calls for a continuous debate. In all means, it is beneficial to keep an eye on HE practices, especially if you desire to be one of the stakeholders.

Indeed, "Information is Power," and I believe you do not have the same perceptions of HE after reading this book, but at least you know what is going on. Importantly, you understand some fundamental changes of practices and disputes that you may face in HE. In addition, the reading may have helped you understand what to expect when learning online, in a physical setting, individually or collaboratively. Likewise, you have obtained information on different contents to learn and challenges that may come your way, as a stumbling block if you do not prepare before heading for a degree. Therefore, take time to think critically on whether you have what it takes to be a student, make an investigation, and prepare yourself in many ways academically, socially, and financially before joining HE. Then, ultimately, contact the university of your choice when you are ready, the one with all you need to succeed to accomplish your degree dream.

I wish you all the best; yes, "Information is Power."

All You Need to

Know Before

Commencing

Higher Education

Appendixes
Appendix 1

Searches related to scholarships (just an example)

https://www.scholarships.com

http://www.scholarships.net.in

http://www.scholarshipsinusa.com.

https://www.scholarships in Canada

https://www.scholarships in norway for international students 2021

https://www.scholarships for international students

For those who desire studying in Australia can search

https://www.studiesinaustralia.com/enquiry-
general?gclid=EAIaIQobChMIu_nYjZrm8gIV2PZRCh0gMAvnEAAYASAA
EgLXVPD_BwE

Or you can go direct to;

http://www.scholars4dev.com/21597/enjoy-your-masters-online-with-
university-of-
southwales/?utm_source=feedburner&utm_medium=email&utm_campaign=Fe

ed%3A+scholars4dev+%28Scholarships+for+Development+%7C+Internationa
l+Scholarships+for+Developing+Countries%29

Alternatively.

https://www.info.com/serp?q=abroad%20scholarships&segment=info.0415&s1
aid=6307071117&s1cid=11388360214&s1agid=109867524845&s1kid=kwd-1
Indeed, from these web pages, you can navigate into different other pages with
diverse scholarship information. mind this is an example and the information can
change so one should learn how to search for information and not the information
itself.

Appendix 2

Some of the Motivational Speakers about education from YouTube (to
mention a few)
TED motivational speakers can be fascinating and others like in the following
pages;

https://www.youtube.com/results?search_query=the+benefits+of+Higher+Educ
ation

https://www.youtube.com/results?search_query=higher+education

https://www.youtube.com/results?search_query=economic+benefit+of+higher+
education.

https://www.youtube.com/results?search_query=Why+higher+education+

https://www.youtube.com/results?search_query=Why+a+degree

These are examples, but one can write whatever he wishes on YouTube or other
media channels and obtain information. However, the challenge is how to filter
the information from irrelevant and relevant.

Appendix 3

Unstructured Interview questions

These are questions I asked the participants who *shared information* written *in this* book.

What makes you think you need a degree?

What do you desire to acquire through the degree you are undertaking?

What is the consequences family encounter by supporting their member for HE?

Why do you think people enrol in higher education?

Do you think there are any practical changes from traditional HE to the current one?

Do you understand what students in HE learn?

Which one is more effective, physical learning or digital?

How can you recognize individual work?

Are there ways to identify plagiarism?

What are the consequences of plagiarism to students?

Are you aware of how the learning is organized?

Who do you think are the main learning agencies in HE?

What are the major learning contents?

What is the importance of having international students in this institution?

What are your comments about government involvement in HE learning and funding?

How many students can be supervised by one supervisor in this university?

What kind of qualifications do tutors/teachers and supervisors must-have?

Do supervisors supervise according to their expertise?

Do you think students understand you? What are the most challenges you have encountered in supervision?

What skills do you think Higher education institutions enhance?

What skills do you think are important to acquire?

Are you aware of the challenges facing higher education today?

What are the challenges?

What do you think the stakeholders should do to enhance learning in higher education?

References

Adams, N. E. (2015). Bloom's taxonomy of cognitive learning objectives. *Journal of the Medical Library Association: JMLA, 103*(3), 152.

Aitchison, C., & Guerin, C. (2014). *Writing groups for doctoral education and beyond: Innovations in practice and theory* Abingdon, Oxon; New York: Routledge.

Amundsen, C., & McAlpine, L. (2009). 'Learning supervision': Trial by fire. *Innovations in Education and Teaching International, 46*(3), 331-342. doi:10.1080/14703290903068805

Amundsen, C., & Wilson, M. (2012). Are we asking the right questions? *Review of Educational Research, 82*(1), 90-126. doi:10.3102/0034654312438409

Anderson, L. W., & Krathwohl, D. R. (2001). *A taxonomy for learning, teaching, and assessing: A revision of Bloom's taxonomy of educational objectives.* Longman.

Anderson, V., & Caldwell, C. (2017). Transformative ethics and trust: The keys to a competitive advantage. *Competitive Advantage: Strategies Management, and Performance, NOVA Publishing, New York,* 133-146.

Barratt-Pugh, L. G., & Krestelica, D. (2018). Bullying in higher education: Culture change requires more than policy. *Perspectives: Policy and Practice in Higher Education,* 1-6.

Barron, A. B., Hebets, E. A., Cleland, T. A., Fitzpatrick, C. L., Hauber, M. E., & Stevens, J. R. (2015). Embracing multiple definitions of learning. *Trends in Neurosciences, 38*(7), 405-407. doi:10.1016/j.tins.2015.04.008

Batliwala, S. (1994a). The meaning of women's empowerment: New concepts from action. *Population policies reconsidered: Health, empowerment and rights, 17*.

Batliwala, S. (1994b). The meaning of women" s empowerment: new concepts from action, in: G. Sen; A. Germain and LC Chen (eds) population policies reconsidered: health, empowerment and rights.

Bell-Ellison, B., & Dedrick, R. F. (2008). What do doctoral students value in their ideal mentor? *Research in Higher Education, 49*(6), 555-567. doi:10.1007/s11162-008-9085-8

Berg, B. L. (2009). In Allyn & Bacon (Ed.), *Qualitative research methods for the social sciences* (7th ed). Boston: Allyn & Bacon. doi:no

Bergman, M. M. (2008). *Advances in mixed methods research* (1st ed.). GB: Sage Publications Ltd. Retrieved from http://replace-me/ebraryid=10504502

Bernard, J. M., & Goodyear, R. K. (2005). of Clinical Supervision. *Supervision in Counseling: Interdisciplinary Issues and Research, 24*(1-2), 3.

Berry, J. W. (2003). *Conceptual approaches to acculturation.* American Psychological Association.

Besti, R. N. (2006). Communication skills training as part of a problem-based learning curriculum. *Journal of Nursing Education, 45*(10), 421.

Bethany A. Bell-Ellison, & Robert F. Dedrick. (2008). What do doctoral students value in their ideal mentor? *Research in Higher Education, 49*(6), 555-567. doi:10.1007/s11162-008-9085-8

Blumenthal, P. (1996). *Academic mobility in a changing world: Regional and global trends. higher education policy 29*. ERIC.

Bone, J. (2007). *Everyday spirituality supporting the spiritual experience of young children in three early childhood educational settings:* Massey University, *New Zealand*

Boud, D., & Lee, A. (2005). 'Peer learning' as a pedagogic discourse for research education 1. *Studies in Higher Education, 30*(5), 501-516.

Boud, D., & Lee, A. (2009). *Changing practices of doctoral education*. London; Routledge.

Bourdieu, P. (1990). *The logic of practice*. Stanford university press.

Bourdieu, P. (2013). *Distinction: A social critique of the judgment of taste*. U.K: Routledge.

Bowen, W. G. (2013). *Higher education in the digital age*. USA: Princeton University Press.

Braathe, H. J., & Otterstad, A. M. (2014). Education for all in Norway: Unpacking quality and equity. *Procedia-Social and Behavioral Sciences, 116*, 1193-1200.

Bridgstock, R. (2009). The graduate attributes we've overlooked: Enhancing graduate employability through career management skills. *Higher Education Research & Development, 28*(1), 31. doi:10.1080/07294360802444347

Burke, P., & Krey, R. D. (2005). *Supervision: A guide to instructional leadership* Charles C Thomas Publisher.

Butler, M. (2016). Equality and anti-discrimination law: The equality act 2010 and other anti-discrimination protections London, England: Spiramus Press.

Byrne, D. (1979). *Teaching writing skills*. Longman, London.

Carter, S. (2014). *Developing generic support for doctoral students: Practice and pedagogy.* New York: Routledge.

Carter, S., Blumenstein, M., & Cook, C. (2013). *Different for women? the challenges of doctoral studies.* UK: doi://doi-org.ezproxy.auckland.ac.nz/10.1080/13562517.2012.719159

Carter, S., & Kumar, V. (2017). 'Ignoring me is part of learning': Supervisory feedback on doctoral writing. *Innovations in Education and Teaching International, 54*(1), 68-75.

Cassell, M. A. (2011). Bullying in academe: Prevalent, significant, and incessant. *Contemporary Issues in Education Research, 4*(5), 33-44.

Chambers, C. R. (2011). *Support systems and services for diverse populations considering the intersection of race, gender, and the needs of black female undergraduates.* Bingley, U.K.: Emerald

Chatterjee, A., & Krishnan, V. R. (2007). Impact of spirituality and political skills on transformational leadership. *Great Lakes Herald, 1*(1), 20-38.

Chiappetta, C., & Watt, S. (2011). Good practice in the supervision & mentoring of postgraduate students: It takes an academy to raise a scholar. Hamilton: McMaster University.

http://docplayer.net/17981364-It-takes-an-academy-to-raise-a-scholar.html

Clark, W. (2007). In ebrary I. (Ed.), *Academic charisma and the origins of the research university.* Chicago: University of Chicago Press.

CLES. (2017). Bullying in different nations. Retrieved from https://laringsmiljosenteret.uis.no/about-us/news/bullying-in-different-nations-article115878-22175.html

Coleman, K. W. (2017). *Diversity's promise for higher education: Making it work by Daryl G. smith (review)* doi:10.1353/csd.2017.0010

Collins, C. S. (2007). A general agreement on higher education: GATS, globalization, and imperialism. *Research in Comparative and International Education, 2*(4), 283-296.

Connell, R. (2015). The knowledge economy and university workers. *Australian Universities' Review, 57*(2), 91-95.

Connell, R., & Manathunga, C. (2012). On doctoral education: How to supervise a Ph.D., 1985-2011. *Australian Universities' Review, The, 54*(1), 5-9.

Craswell, G. (2007). Deconstructing the skills training debate in doctoral education. *Higher Education Research & Development, 26*(4), 377-391.

Crebert, G., Bates, M., Bell, B., Patrick, C., & Cragnolini, V. (2004). Developing generic skills at university, during work placement and in employment: graduates' perceptions. *Higher Education Research & Development, 23*(2), 147-165. doi:10.1080/0729436042000206636

Creswell, J. W., Plano Clark, V. L., Gutmann, M. L., & Hanson, W. E. (2003). An expanded typology for classifying mixed methods research into designs. *A. Tashakkori y C. Teddlie, Handbook of mixed methods in social and behavioural research*, 209-240.

Creswell, J. W. (2015). *A concise introduction to mixed methods research.* Los Angeles: SAGE.

Creswell, J. W. (2018a). In Poth C. N. (Ed.), *Qualitative inquiry & research design: Choosing among five approaches* (4th ed.). Los Angeles: SAGE.

Creswell, J. W. (2018b). In Creswell J. D. (Ed.), *Research design: Qualitative, quantitative & mixed methods approach* (5th edition. International student edition.. ed.). Los Angeles: SAGE.

Creswell, J. W., & Plano Clark, V. L. (2007). In Plano Clark V. L. (Ed.), *Designing and conducting mixed methods research*. Thousand Oaks, Calif.: SAGE.

Creswell, J. W., & Plano Clark, V. L. (2011). In Plano Clark V. L. (Ed.), *Designing and conducting mixed methods research* (2nd. ed.). Los Angeles: SAGE.

Creswell, J. W., & Plano Clark, V. L. (2018). In Plano Clark V. L. (Ed.), *Designing and conducting mixed methods research* (3rd ed.). USA: SAGE.

Creswell, J. W., Plano Clark, V. L., Gutmann, M. L., & Hanson, W. E. (2003). Advanced mixed methods research designs. *Handbook of Mixed Methods in Social and Behavioral Research, 209,* 240.

Czinkota, M., & Ronkainen, I. (2011). 4 academic freedom for all in higher education: The role of the general agreement on trade in services. *The future of global business* (pp. 74-98) Routledge.

Dalziel, P. (2017). Education and qualifications as skills. *The Oxford Handbook of Skills and Training,* 143. UK.

Devos, C., Boudrenghien, G., Van der Linden, N., Azzi, A., Frenay, M., Galand, B., & Klein, O. (2017). Doctoral students' experiences leading to completion or attrition: A matter of sense, progress, and distress. *European Journal of Psychology of Education, 32*(1), 61-77.

Doyle, S., Manathunga, C., Prinsen, G., Tallon, R., & Cornforth, S. (2017). African international doctoral students in New Zealand: Englishes, doctoral writing and intercultural supervision. *Higher Education Research & Development*, 1-14.

Duflo, E. (2012). Women empowerment and economic development. *Journal of Economic Literature, 50*(4), 1051-1079.

Eley, A., & Jennings, R. (2005). *Effective postgraduate supervision: Improving the student/supervisor relationship: Improving the student/supervisor relationship* McGraw-Hill Education (UK).

Eraut, M. (2004). Informal learning in the workplace. *Studies in Continuing Education, 26*(2), 247-273.

EURASHE (European Ministers in charge of Higher Education). (2016). *The bologna declaration of 19 June 1999: Joint declaration of the European ministers of education.* 689: EURASHE. doi://www.eurashe.EU/library/bologna_1999_bologna-declaration-pdf/

Eustace, J., Baird, K., Saito, A. S., & Creedy, D. K. (2016). Midwives' experiences of routine inquiry for intimate partner violence in pregnancy. *Women and Birth, 29*(6), 503-510.

Evans, C., & Waring, M. (2011). Student-teacher assessment feedback preferences: The influence of cognitive styles and gender. *Learning and Individual Differences, 21*(3), 271-280.

B.F. skinner. Part 1. Evans, Richard I (Richard Isadore) and Skinner, B. F. (. (Directors). (1964). [Video/DVD] University Park, PA: University Park, PA: Penn State Media 1964.

Fan, X., & Chen, M. (2001). Parental involvement and students' academic achievement: A meta-analysis. *Educational psychology review, 13* (1), 1-22.

Floyd, C. B. (2011). Critical thinking in a second language. *Higher Education Research & Development, 30*(3), 289-302. doi:10.1080/07294360.2010.501076

Freire, P., & Fraser, J. W. (1997). *Mentoring the mentor: A critical dialogue with Paulo Freire.* New York: New York: P. Lang c1997.

Fusch, P. I., & Ness, L. R. (2015). Are we there yet? Data saturation in qualitative research. *The Qualitative Report, 20* (9), 1408-1416.

Gibbs, G. R. (2018). *Analyzing qualitative data.* (Vol. 6). Sage.

Gokhberg, L., Meissner, D., & Shmatko, N. (2017). Myths and realities of highly qualified labour and what it means for PhDs. *Journal of the Knowledge Economy, 8* (2), 758-767.

Golde, C. M. (2000). Should I stay or should I go? student descriptions of the doctoral attrition process. *The Review of Higher Education, 23* (2), 199-227.

Golding, C., Sharmini, S., & Lazarovitch, A. (2014). What examiners do: what thesis students should know. *Assessment & Evaluation in Higher Education, 39* (5), 563-576.

Goldthorpe, J. H. (2007). "Cultural capital": Some critical observations. *Sociologica, 1* (2), 0-0.

Graff, C., J., Russell, K., C., & Stegbauer, C., C. (2007). Formative and summative evaluation of a practice doctorate program. *Nurse Educator, 32* (4), 173-177. doi:10.1097/01.NNE.0000281088.81205.24

Grant, B. (2003). Mapping the pleasures and risks of supervision. *Discourse: Studies in the Cultural Politics of Education, 24*(2), 175-190. doi:10.1080/01596300303042

Grant, B. M. (2005a). *The pedagogy of graduate supervision: Figuring the relations between supervisor and student* (Doctoral dissertation, ResearchSpace@ Auckland).

Grant, B. M. (2005b). Fighting for space in supervision: Fantasies, fairy tales, fictions, and fallacies. *International Journal of Qualitative Studies in Education, 18* (3), 337-354. doi:10.1080/09518390500082483

Grant, B. M. (2008). Agonistic struggle: Master-slave dialogues in humanities supervision. *Arts and Humanities in Higher Education, 7* (1), 9-27.

Grant, B., & Manathunga, C. (2011). Supervision and cultural difference: Rethinking institutional pedagogies. *Innovations in Education and Teaching International, 48* (4), 351-354. doi:10.1080/14703297.2011.617084

Grant, B., & Mckinley, E. (2011). Coloring the pedagogy of doctoral supervision: Considering supervisor, student, and knowledge through the lens of indigeneity. *Innovations in Education and Teaching International, 48* (4), 377-386. doi:10.1080/14703297.2011.617087

Greenberg, R. D. (2018). Making universities grow: The New Zealand experience. *Sustainable futures for higher education* (pp. 99-107) Springer.

Guerin, C., Carter, S., & Aitchison, C. (2015). Blogging as a community of practice: Lessons for academic development? *International Journal for Academic Development, 20* (3), 212-223. doi:10.1080/1360144X.2015.1042480

Guri-Rosenblit, S., Šebková, H., & Teichler, U. (2007). Massification and diversity of higher education systems: Interplay of complex dimensions. *Higher Education Policy, 20* (4), 373-389.

Hall, L. A., & Burns, L. D. (2009). Identity development and mentoring in doctoral education. *Harvard Educational Review, 79* (1), 49-70.

Halse, C. (2011). 'Becoming a supervisor': The impact of doctoral supervision on supervisors' learning. *Studies in Higher Education, 36* (5), 557-570. doi:10.1080/03075079.2011.594593

Halse, C., & Malfroy, J. (2010). Retheorizing doctoral supervision as professional work. *Studies in Higher Education, 35* (1), 79-92. doi:10.1080/03075070902906798

Helguero-Balcells, G. (2009). The Bologna declaration agreement impact on US higher education: Recommendations for integration. *International Journal of Learning, 16* (10).

Herd, C., & Moore, R. (2012). Multicultural issues: Supervision and multicultural issues: Supervisors and supervisees. *SIG 11 Perspectives on Administration and Supervision, 22*(1), 33-39.

Hillman, N. W., Tandberg, D. A., & Fryar, A. H. (2015). Evaluating the impacts of "new" performance funding in higher education. *Educational Evaluation and Policy Analysis, 37* (4), 501-519. doi:10.3102/0162373714560224

Johansson, T., Wisker, G., Claesson, S., Strandler, O., & Saalman, E. (2014). Ph.D. supervision as an emotional process – critical situations and emotional boundary work. *Pertanika Journal of Social Science and Humanities, 22* (2), 605-620.

Johnson, B., & Christensen, L. (2008). *Educational Research: Quantitative, qualitative, and mixed approaches*. Sage.

Jones, G. A. (2014). An introduction to higher education in Canada. *Higher Education Across Nations, 1*, 1-38.

Keashly, L., & Neuman, J. H. (2013). Bullying in higher education. *Workplace Bullying in Higher Education,* 1-22.

Keefer, J. M. (2015). Experiencing doctoral liminality as a conceptual threshold and how supervisors can use it. *Innovations in Education and Teaching International, 52* (1), 17-28.

Keeling, R. (2006). The bologna process and the Lisbon research agenda: The European commission's expanding role in higher education discourse. *European Journal of Education, 41*(2), 203-223.

Kelly, F. (2010). Reflecting on the purpose of the Ph.D. oral examination. *New Zealand Journal of Educational Studies, 45* (1), 77.

Kelly, F. (2017). *The idea of the Ph.D. The doctorate in the twenty-first-century imagination*. New York: Routledge.

Kidman, J., Manathunga, C., & Cornforth, S. (2017). Intercultural Ph.D. supervision: Exploring the hidden curriculum in a social science faculty doctoral program. *Higher Education Research & Development,* 1-14.

Kiley, M. (2011a). Developments in research supervisor training: Causes and responses. *Studies in Higher Education, 36* (5), 585-599. doi:10.1080/03075079.2011.594595

Kiley, M. (2011b). Government policy and research higher degree of education. *Journal of Higher Education Policy and Management, 33* (6), 629-640. doi:10.1080/1360080X.2011.621189

Kiley, M., & Mullins, G. (2005). Supervisors' conceptions of research: What are they? *Scandinavian Journal of Educational Research, 49* (3), 245-262. doi:10.1080/00313830500109550

Kiley, M., & Wisker, G. (2010). Learning to be a researcher: The concepts and crossings. *Threshold concepts and transformational learning* () Sense Publishers.

Kivinen, O., & Ahola, S. (1999). Higher education as human risk capital. *Higher Education, 38* (2), 191-208.

Kivinen, O., Hedman, J., & Kaipainen, P. (2007). From elite university to mass higher education: Educational expansion, equality of opportunity and returns to university education. *Acta Sociologica, 50* (3), 231-247.

Kiyama, J. M., & Rios-Aguilar, C. (2017). A complementary framework: Funds of knowledge and the forms of capital. *Funds of knowledge in higher education* (pp. 7-24) Routledge.

Kostrykina, S., Lee, K., & Hope, J. (2017). The west, the rest and the knowledge economy: A game worth playing? *Perspectives: Policy and Practice in Higher Education,* 1-10.

Krathwohl, D. R. (2002). A revision of bloom's taxonomy: An overview. *Theory into Practice, 41*(4), 212-218.

Lapan, C., Hodge, C., Peroff, D., & Henderson, K. (2013). Female faculty in higher education: The politics of hope? Schole, 28(2), n/a. doi:10.1080/1937156X.2013.11949702

Laufer, M., & Gorup, M. (2019). The invisible others: Stories of international doctoral student dropout. *Higher Education, 78* (1), 165-181.

Lee, A., & Danby, S. (2012). *Reshaping doctoral education: International approaches and pedagogies.* Abingdon, Oxon; New York: Routledge.

Lee, A., & Dunston, R. (2011). Practice, learning, and change: Towards a re-theorization of professional education. *Teaching in Higher Education, 16* (5), 483-494. doi:10.1080/13562517.2011.580840

Lee, A., & Green, B. (2009). Supervision as metaphor. *Studies in Higher Education, 34* (6), 615-630.

Lee, A., & Kamler, B. (2008). Bringing pedagogy to doctoral publishing. *Teaching in Higher Education, 13* (5), 511-523. doi:10.1080/13562510802334723

Lee, A. (2008). How are doctoral students supervised? concepts of doctoral research supervision. *Studies in Higher Education, 33* (3), 267-281. doi:10.1080/03075070802049202

Lee, A. M. (2007). Developing effective supervisors: Concepts of research supervision. *South African Journal of Higher Education, 21* (4), 680-693.

Lesley Cooper, Janice Orrell, & Margaret Bowden. (2010). *Work-integrated learning* (1st ed.). London: Routledge Ltd. doi:10.4324/9780203854501 Retrieved from http://www.tandfebooks.com/isbn/9780203854501

Lever-Duffy, J. (2008). In McDonald J. B., Ciereszko A. A. and Mizell A. P. (Eds.), *Teaching and learning with technology* (3rd ed.. ed.). Boston, MA: Boston, MA: Pearson/Allyn and Bacon.

Li, Q. (2006). Cyberbullying in schools: A research of gender differences. *School Psychology International, 27* (2), 157-170.

Lillejord, S., Børte, K., Nesje, K., & Ruud, E. (2018). Learning and teaching with technology in higher education–a systematic review. *Oslo: Knowledge Center for Education,*

Lindsey, L. L. (2015). *Gender roles: A sociological perspective* (4th ed.). Upper Saddle Upper Saddle River, N.J. : Pearson Prentice Hall.

Lindsey, L. L. (2015). The sociology of gender theoretical perspectives and feminist frameworks. In *Gender roles* (pp. 23-48). Routledge.

Lopez-Claros, A., Zahidi, S., & Forum économique mondial. (2005, May). Women's empowerment: Measuring the global gender gap. Geneva: World Economic Forum.

Lovas, S. (1980). Higher degree examination procedures in Australian universities. *Vestes, 23* (1), 9-13.

Lund, E. M., & Ross, S. W. (2017). Bullying perpetration, victimization, and demographic differences in college students: A review of the literature. *Trauma, Violence, & Abuse, 18* (3), 348-360.

Maassen, P., Nokkala, T., & Uppstrm, T. M. (2004). Internationalization of higher education institutions in northern Europe in the light of bologna-national and institutional case studies.

Madan, A. (2018). Rethinking human capital. *NHRD Network Journal, 11* (1), 25-29.

Manathunga, C. (2005). The development of research supervision: "Turning the light on a private space". *International Journal for Academic Development, 10* (1), 17-30.

Manathunga, C. (2009). Research as an intercultural "contact zone". *Discourse: Studies in the Cultural Politics of Education, 30*(2), 165-177. doi:10.1080/01596300902809161

Manathunga, C. (2017). Intercultural doctoral supervision: The centrality of place, time and other forms of knowledge. *Arts and Humanities in Higher Education, 16* (1), 113-124.

Manathunga, C., Guilherme, M., & Dietz, G. (2017). Intercultural doctoral supervision: The centrality of place, time and other forms of knowledge. *Arts and Humanities in Higher Education, 16* (1), 113-124. doi:10.1177/1474022215580119

Manathunga, C., Lant, P., & Mellick, G. (2006). Imagining an interdisciplinary doctoral pedagogy. *Teaching in Higher Education, 11* (3), 365-379.

Manathunga, C., Lant, P., & Mellick, G. (2007). Developing professional researchers: Research students' graduate attributes. *Studies in Continuing Education, 29* (1), 19-36.

Marek, K., & Peter, M. (2012). *National higher education reforms in a European context: Comparative reflections on Poland and Norway* Peter Lang.

Marginson, S., & van der Wende, M. (2009). Europeanisation, international rankings, and faculty mobility: Three cases in higher education globalization. *Higher Education To, 2030*, 109-141.

Maringe, F., & Foskett, N. (2012). *Globalization and internationalization in higher education: Theoretical, strategic and management perspectives* A&C Black.

Marzano, R. J., Frontier, T., & Livingston, D. (2011). *Effective supervision: Supporting the art and science of teaching.* Google: Ascd.

McAdam, M., Harrison, R. T., & Leitch, C. M. (2018). Stories from the field: Women networking as gender capital in entrepreneurial ecosystems. *Small Business Economics,* 1-16.

McAlpine, L. (2012). Identity-trajectories: Doctoral journeys from past to present to future. *Australian Universities' Review, The, 54* (1), 38.

McAlpine, L., & Amundsen, C. (2012). Challenging the taken-for-granted: How to research analysis might inform pedagogical practices and institutional policies related to doctoral education. *Studies in Higher Education, 37* (6), 683-694. doi:10.1080/03075079.2010.537747

McAlpine, L., & Amundsen, C. (2016). Achieved research-teaching (non-research routes). *Post-PhD career trajectories* (pp. 51-58) Springer.

McCornack, S. (2015). Information manipulation theory. The International Encyclopedia of Interpersonal Communication, 1-7.

McMillan, J. (2005). Course change and attrition from higher education. *LSAY Research Reports,* 43.

MoENZ. (2015). *Tertiary education strategy 2014 – 2019.* Australia: Australian

Government webpage. https://www.education.govt.nz/further-education/policies-and-strategies/tertiary-education-strategy/

MoETE. (2017). Tertiary education strategies 2014-2019 The Ministry of Education Tertiary. https://www.education.govt.nz/assets/Documents/Further-education/Tertiary-Education-Strategy.pdf

Boyle, D. M., Carpenter, B. W., & Mahoney, D. P. (2017). Developing the communication skills required for sustainable career success. *Management Accounting Quarterly (Fall)*, 1-9.

Morgan, D. L., Eliot, S., Lowe, R. A., & Gorman, P. (2016). Dyadic interviews as a tool for qualitative evaluation. *American Journal of Evaluation, 37* (1), 109-117. doi:10.1177/1098214015611244

Mowbray, S., & Halse, C. (2010). The purpose of the Ph.D.: Theorising the skills acquired by students. *Higher Education Research & Development, 29* (6), 653-664. doi:10.1080/07294360.2010.487199

Murphy, N. (2009). Research supervision: Matches and mismatches. *International Journal of Electrical Engineering Education, 46* (3), 295-306. doi:10.7227/IJEEE.46.3.7

Nada, C. I., & Araújo, H. C. (2018). 'When you welcome students without borders, you need a mentality without borders' internationalization of higher education: Evidence from Portugal. *Studies in Higher Education,* 1-14.

Neveu, E. (2018). Bourdieu's capital (s). *The oxford handbook of Pierre Bourdieu* (pp. 347) Oxford University Press.

Noble, H., & Smith, J. (2015). Issues of validity and reliability in qualitative research. *Evidence-Based Nursing, 18* (2), 34-35.

OECD. (2018). *Higher education in Norway labour market relevance and outcomes.* Paris: OECD.

Onwuegbuzie, A. J., Dickinson, W. B., Leech, N. L., & Zoran, A. G. (2009). A qualitative framework for collecting and analysing data in focus group research. *International Journal of Qualitative Methods, 8* (3), 1-21.

Onwuegbuzie, A. J., Frels, R. K., Leech, N. L., & Collins, K. M. (2011). A mixed research study of pedagogical approaches and student learning in doctoral-level mixed research courses. *International Journal of Multiple Research Approaches, 5* (2), 169-199. doi:10.5172/mra.2011.5.2.169

Overtoom, C. (2000). Employability skills: An update. ERIC digest no. 220.

Palmer, R. T., Davis, R. J., & Gasman, M. (2011). A matter of diversity, equity, and necessity: The tension between Maryland's higher education system and its historically black colleges and universities over the office of civil rights agreement. *The Journal of Negro Education,* 121-133.

Palmer, W. (2012). *Discovering arguments: An introduction to critical thinking, writing, and style* (4th ed.. ed.). Boston: Pearson Prentice Hall.

Park, C. (2007). Redefining the doctorate. *The Higher Education Academy, Discussion Paper* doi://eprints.lancs.ac.uk/id

Pedersen, H. S. (2014). New doctoral graduates in the knowledge economy: Trends and key issues. *Journal of Higher Education Policy and Management, 36* (6), 632-645. doi:10.1080/1360080X.2014.957891

Pla-Julián, I., & Díez, J. (2019). Equality plans and gender perception in university students. *Mediterranean Journal of Social Sciences, 10* (4), 39-52.

Posselt, T., Abdelkafi, N., Fischer, L., & Tangour, C. (2019). Opportunities and challenges of higher education institutions in Europe: An analysis from a business model perspective. *Higher Education Quarterly,*

Powell, I. (2013). Can you see me? experiences of nurses working the night shift in Australian regional hospitals: A qualitative case study. *Journal of Advanced Nursing, 69* (10), 2172-2184.

Price, S., & Rogers, Y. (2004). Let's get physical: The learning benefits of interacting in digitally augmented physical spaces. *Computers & Education, 43* (1-2), 137-151.

Rossi, F. (2010). Massification, competition and organizational diversity in higher education: Evidence from Italy. *Studies in Higher Education, 35* (3), 277-300. doi:10.1080/03075070903050539

Ryan, R. M., & Deci, E. L. (2000). Self-determination theory and the facilitation of intrinsic motivation, social development, and well-being. *American Psychologist, 55* (1), 68.

Sawir, E. (2011). Dealing with diversity in internationalized higher education institutions. *Intercultural Education, 22* (5), 381-394. doi:10.1080/14675986.2011.643136

Schultz, T. W. (1974). *Economics of the family; marriage, children and human capital; a conference report.* University of Chicago Press, Chicago, US.

Sheehan, J. (1994). External examiners: Roles and issues. *Journal of Advanced Nursing, 20* (5), 943-949. doi:10.1046/j.1365-2648.1994.20050943.

Simpson, R. (1983). *How the Ph.D. came to Britain. A century of struggle for postgraduate education. SRHE monograph 54.* U.K: ERIC.

Simpson, T. L. (2010). Regional stewardship and the redefinition of higher education. *Philosophical Studies in Education, 41,* 106-115.

Siedentop, D., Hastie, P., & Van der Mars, H. (2019). *Complete guide to sport education.* Human Kinetics.

Slonje, R., & Smith, P. K. (2008). Cyberbullying: Another main type of bullying? *Scandinavian Journal of Psychology, 49*(2), 147-154.

Sluijsmans, D., Dochy, F., & Moerkerke, G. (1998). Creating a learning environment by using self-, peer-and co-assessment. *Learning Environments Research, 1* (3), 293-319.

Spriggs, A. L., Iannotti, R. J., Nansel, T. R., & Haynie, D. L. (2007). Adolescent bullying involvement and perceived family, peer and school relations: Commonalities and differences across race/ethnicity. *Journal of Adolescent Health, 41* (3), 283-293.

Stensaker, B. (2006). Governmental policy, organizational ideals and institutional adaptation in Norwegian higher education. *Studies in Higher Education, 31* (1), 43-56.

Stensaker, B., Frolich, N., Gornitzka, A., & Maassen, P. (2008). Internationalization of higher education: The gap between national policy-making and institutional needs. *Globalization, Societies, and Education, 6* (1), 1-11. doi:10.1080/14767720701855550

Sweetland, S. R. (1996). Human capital theory: Foundations of a field of inquiry. *Review of Educational Research, 66* (3), 341-359.

Taylor, R. (2015). Beyond anonymity: Temporality and the production of knowledge in a qualitative longitudinal study. *International Journal of Social Research Methodology, 18* (3), 281-292. doi:10.1080/13645579.2015.1017901

Tholen, G. (2014). Graduate employability and educational context: A comparison between Great Britain and the Netherlands. *British Educational Research Journal, 40* (1), 1-17.

Tholen, G. (2017). *Graduate work: Skills, credentials, careers, and labour markets* (First edition.. ed.). Paris: Oxford: Oxford University Press.

Thomas, D. G., Chinn, P., Perkins, F., & Carter, D. G. (1994). Multicultural education: Reflections on brown at 40. *The Journal of Negro Education, 63* (3), 460-469.

Throsby, D. (1999). Cultural capital. *Journal of Cultural Economics, 23* (1-2), 3-12.

Toulson, R. G. (2006). In Phipps C. M. (Ed.), *Confidentiality* (2nd ed.). London: London: Sweet & Maxwell.

Underwood, S. J., & Austin, C. E. (2016). Higher education graduate preparation programs: Characteristics and trends. *Journal of College Student Development, 57* (3), 326-332. doi:10.1353/csd.2016.0028

United Nations. (1975). World conference of the international women's year Mexico City world conference.

United Nations. (1985). World conference to review and appraise the achievements of the united nations decade for women: Equality, development and world conference 2.

United Nations. (1995). Action for equality, development and peace Beijing, Beijing declaration.

UiO (2021) Another route to a doctoral degree.
https://www.uio.no/english/research/phd/drphilos/

Usher, A., & Savino, M. (2006). A world of difference: A global survey of university league tables. Canadian education report series. *Online Submission,*

Usher, R. (2002). A diversity of doctorates: Fitness for the knowledge economy? *Higher Education Research & Development, 21* (2), 143-153. doi:10.1080/07294360220144060

Valimaa, J., & Hoffman, D. (2008). Knowledge society discourse and higher education. *Higher Education: The International Journal of Higher Education and Educational Planning, 56* (3), 265-285. doi:10.1007/s10734-008-9123-7

Van der Wende, M. (2007). Internationalization of higher education in the OECD countries: Challenges and opportunities for the coming decade. *Journal of Studies in International Education, 11* (3-4), 274-289.

Van Der Wende, M. (2015). International academic mobility: Towards a concentration of the minds in Europe. *European Review, 23* (S1), S7-S88.

Walker, M., & Thomson, P. (Eds.). (2010). *The Routledge doctoral supervisor's companion: Supporting effective research in education and the social sciences.* Routledge.

Weigel, F. K., & Bonica, M. (2014). An active learning approach to bloom's taxonomy. *U.S.Army Medical Department Journal*, 21-29.

Whitney, I., & Smith, P. K. (1993). A survey of the nature and extent of bullying in junior/middle and secondary schools. *Educational Research, 35* (1), 3-25.

Wiles, R., Crow, G., Heath, S., & Charles, V. (2008). The management of confidentiality and anonymity in social research. *International Journal of Social Research Methodology, 11* (5), 417-428.

Wisker, G. (2005). *The good supervisor: Supervising postgraduate and undergraduate research for doctoral theses and dissertations.* New York: Macmillan.

Wisker, G. (2012). *The good supervisor: Supervising postgraduate and undergraduate research for doctoral theses and dissertations.* U.K: Palgrave Macmillan.

Wisker, G. (2015). *Getting published: MA26 publishing success.* U.K: Macmillan International Higher Education.

Wisker, G., Kiley, M., & Masika, R. (2016). Threshold crossings and doctoral education: Learning from the examination of doctoral education.

Wisker, G., & Robinson, G. (2014). Examiner practices and culturally inflected doctoral theses. *Discourse: Studies in the Cultural Politics of Education, 35* (2), 190-205. doi:10.1080/01596306.2012.745730

Wisker, G., & Robinson, G. (2015). Experiences of the creative doctorate: Minstrels and white lines. *Critical Studies in Teaching and Learning, 2* (2) doi:10.14426/cristal.v2i2.36

Wisker, G., Robinson, G., Trafford, V., Lilly, J., & Warnes, M. (2004). Achieving a doctorate: Meta-learning and research development programs supporting success for international distance students. *Innovations in Education and Teaching International, 41* (4), 473-489. doi:10.1080/1470329042000277048.

Wisker, G. & Robinson, G. (2016). Supervisor wellbeing and identity: Challenges and strategies. *International Journal for Researcher Development, 7* (2), 123-140.

Wolff, L. (2010). Learning through writing: Reconceptualising the research supervision process. *International Journal of Teaching and Learning in Higher Education, 22* (3), 229-237.

Wu, H., & Zha, Q. (2018). A new typology for analysing the direction of movement in higher education internationalization. *Journal of Studies in International Education, 22* (3), 259-277.

Xu, L., & Grant, B. (2017). International doctoral students' becoming: A dialogic perspective. *Innovations in Education and Teaching International,* 1-10. doi:10.1080/14703297.2017.1318711

Young-Jones, A., Fursa, S., Byrket, J. S., & Sly, J. S. (2015). Bullying affects more than feelings: The long-term implications of victimization on academic motivation in higher education. *Social Psychology of Education, 18* (1), 185-200.

CPSIA information can be obtained
at www.ICGtesting.com
Printed in the USA
BVHW052133170323
660681BV00008B/130